THE WORLD'S FASTEST
MOTORCYCLES

THE WORLD'S FASTEST
MOTORCYCLES

John Cutts &
Michael Scott

Quantum
Books

A QUANTUM BOOK

This book is produced by
Quantum Publishing Ltd.
6 Blundell Street
London N7 9BH

ISBN 1-86160-836-5

QUMWFM

Manufactured in Singapore by
Pica Digital (Pte) Ltd
Printed in Singapore by
Star Standard Industries (Pte) Ltd

CONTENTS

For Learner and Expert

This *is* the golden age of motorcycling. The contemporary motorcycles profiled in this book are the fastest, most powerful two-wheelers of all time – ultimate dream machines with such sparkling specifications and dizzy performance levels that their very existence would have been unimaginable a few years ago. If the 1970s was the era of the original superbikes, the late 1980s will be remembered for the arrival of genuine racing replicas – 160mph racing bikes made into street hardware – motorcycles so awesomely powerful, plain quick and specialized that they are simply authentic racers with headlights. Racing has not only improved the breed but created a new genus of bikes – Grand Prix replica speedballs for the street.

What are they like to ride, these fabulous, fire-breathing roadburners? Despite a top speed capability that is virtually unusable outside a proper race-track, these exotic machines are safer and easier to ride than ever before. There have been huge improvements, not only in engine development and power output but also in the cycle components – the wheels, tyres, frames, suspension and brakes. The bikes are getting lighter yet stronger, more manageable and robust. They handle confidently, steer responsively, brake better and hold the road with impressive authority. Riding a modern sports bike is like flying. Rider and machine are as one, the rider becoming an extension of the motorcycle, hands operating the throttle, steering and brakes, feet selecting gear ratios, the whole body controlling stability and direction, head tucked in down the straights, knee out and dragging in the corners, transferring body weight for the perfect line through every bend. The lure and thrills of the open road on a fast bike are more attractive, exhilarating and intoxicating than ever, offering an irresistible mixture of speed and power, force and momentum, danger tempered with skill and grace. The throttle still goes both ways but it opens wider and gets on the gas harder and quicker these days.

Development has been astonishing. Big bike enthusiasts around the world are bedazzled by the glittering choice of sports weapons now available. The four-stroke market is currently dominated by 160mph litre-plus bikes such as the Suzuki GSX-R1100 and the Yamaha's FZR1000, liquid-cooled in-line fours making 130hp and lots of redline rpm. Their power-to-weight ratios are quite exceptional. The lightweight Yamaha 134hp package weighs just 460lb. This is a power-to-weight ratio simply unobtainable in the car world except at the very highest level of competition. At the top end of the four-stroke market, the state of the art is 175mph – an astonishing top speed recorded by at least two bikes in this book, Kawasaki's mass-produced ZZ-R1100 and Bimota's rather more exclusive, limited edition Tuatara.

The trend is undeniably towards the lighter 750s and 600s though. The best of these will do 150mph and their power, being less fierce, can be nailed to the road more easily.

The cross-over between race bikes and road machines is now complete. People have always raced road bikes in production classes, but now any aspiring private racer can easily and quickly transform an out-of-the-crate road machine into a competitive World Championship Endurance or Formula One mount. Whatever part you look at on a modern bike, the influence of the race-track is obvious. From the aerodynamic lines of the screen to the construction of the few inches of rubber that are the bike's only contact with the road, racing parallels are manifest, enhancing the overall performance. The wheels are smaller and lighter, giving less unsprung weight and quicker steering. The tyres have become fatter, low-profile, wide-section, more adept at holding the road and coping with the wheel-spinning acceleration. Radial tyres are now commonplace on all top dog sports bikes. The brakes feature four-piston calipers biting on floating discs. The forks are large-diameter, often with a brace between the legs to resist flex. Rear suspension is monoshock, which weighs less and rules out the imbalance inevitable with two shock absorbers. The single dampers are fed by a variety of rocking arms and linkages – Uni-Trak, Full-Floater, Pro-Link and Monocross. Some are rising-rate, all are extremely efficient at dealing with the bumps. Ride quality and suspension are probably *the* most significantly improved features of the last ten years of mass-production motorcycles. Finally the manufacturers have realized that *useable* power is more important than out-right power. Suspension, roadholding, handling and comfort are the key areas that have been addressed and generally improved beyond all recognition when compared to how motorcycles used to perform.

Frames, still traditionally the preserve of small specialist builders, are also receiving more attention and design consideration. Double steel cradles are still commonplace but increasingly the trend is towards using the engine as a stressed frame member. Aluminium beam-type frames, as developed and campaigned in Grand Prix races, have naturally found their way onto the street-legal replicas. Aerodynamic studies have paid dividends in making a motorcycle more slippery and streamlined at speed, often against the wind, as it cuts through the air. Fairings, screens, fork legs, mudguards and bodywork are now integrated to achieve the lowest possible drag coefficient. For a big bike an efficient fairing may be worth something like the equivalent of 25bhp and 20mph on its top speed.

Naturally there will always be pure speed engineering – engine development and the relentless pursuit of horsepower. On four-strokes, less than four valves per cylinder is unusual (Yamaha's FZ750 has five) and more valve area means the gas can be worked on faster. Valve trains are still typically chain-driven DOHC but gear-driven cams can be found on Honda's VF750 and RC30. Carburettors come in all shapes and sizes, feeding V4s from inside the vee and in-line fours from above the motor by downdraft induction. Usually they are of compact, constant vacuum design; others have flat sides. All are ultra-responsive under every operating condition. Ignition systems have been completely transistorized for some time – the very best work with computer-controlled digital fuel injection. Exhausts vary from the almost ubiquitous four-into-two with balance pipe, sometimes with complex cross-over headers, to the maximum grunt of four-into-one exhaust plumbing with a large collector. Clutches are increasingly becoming hydraulically operated. Cranks, cams, con rods and pistons are being made lighter yet stronger. The use of exotic, lightweight materials from magnesium or carbon fibre is becoming more affordable and thus more commonplace.

As for horsepower itself, nobody really knows where the ceiling lies. Around the world, safety-conscious watchdogs,

legislators and governments have viewed the escalating horsepower war with alarm. In Europe many countries have adopted a 100bhp limit. In pursuit of power and speed, the major manufacturers may have already paved the way towards the extinction of these ultimate sports machines. Does anybody really need a 160mph road bike?

Meanwhile, motorcycling goes on at the speed of life itself. The bikes in this book were not built as utilitarian commuters or run-arounds, they were constructed around one guiding principle and are united by one single, serious purpose – maximum mph motorcycling. In every red-blooded enthusiast's dream garage, there are a number of motorcycles – one for the street, another for the long tour, a dirt bike perhaps, certainly a flash-looking café racer plus a couple of out-and-out sport tools. The machines on the following pages are strictly the best – the world's fastest and the world's finest. Nothing on the road can live with these bikes. They are in a different league – untouchable, immaculate, unique but also accessible, freely available and relatively cheap. Pull on a helmet, zip up those colour coordinated leathers, take a deep breath, turn the key and go for it. Motorcycling may never be this good again.

RIGHT: In the 1990s real superbikes will get smaller, lighter and put as much emphasis on good handling as on outright power. Suzuki's GSX-R750 is a sports bike that's been around for over 5 years and has been refined to the hilt.

OPPOSITE ABOVE: Bimota's all-action Bellaria uses a tuned Yamaha FZR600 engine in a lightweight, sports-stiff but sharply-responsive chassis.

OPPOSITE BELOW: Kawasaki's ZXR-750 began life as a road bike you could kit out for the race track. By 1990 and the third model of the ZXR, Kawasaki had fitted most of the race kit parts as standard.

SUPERBIKING MILESTONES

The word superbike came out of the 1960s. In one sense it was a cliché, a buzz-word, but in another it was a specific term for an actual concept. A superbike is a machine conceived not for sound reasons of common sense, but in a hedonistic celebration that combines the exhilaration of fine engineering with the wild joy of unfettered speed; a celebration of an excess of horsepower over horse-sense. A superbike is a vehicle that nobody needs but that every dedicated motorcyclist wants.

The concept is older than the word. It has been an intrinsic part of motorcycling since the first sporting gent, his flat cap worn rakishly, peak to the rear, endeavoured to have a single cylinder that chuffed more powerfully than his neighbour's. Once, the legend goes, there were only two motorcycles in the world. The faster was the original superbike.

They were not just reckless toys, those distant Indians and Harleys, those Broughs and Vincents, the Motor Guzzis and the MV Agustas. They have served a broader interest than the thrills of the foolhardy few. As a forcing house for ideas and a field for engineering endeavour they have inevitably borne the fruit of excellence. Once, a twin overhead camshaft design of four cylinders was the epitome of rarity and extravagance of design. Today, the same engine design is common-place on public roads.

There have been glamorous aberrations along the route: Vee-twins in great profusion, asymmetrical three cylinder designs, two-strokes and four-strokes. Even today, the in-line four is not quite the definitive design . . . V3s and V4s, square-fours, and the long-lived Vee-twin all appear amongst the fastest bikes.

By tracing the landmarks of design (including significant deviations) the evolution of the modern superbike becomes clearer. An historical perspective may also make the directions taken by the next generation a bit less surprising.

The modern superbike began with the Brough Superior of the 1930s. It was a machine much like the others of its day, but with something extra. In the fashion of the times, the engine was a proprietary unit, usually a JAP Vee-twin. George Brough, who had a keen eye for what would make his machines stand out, made the rest. He included some fine detail engineering, plenty of spit and polish, and engine tuning to ensure a good turn of speed. There was nothing *mechanically* outstanding about the machines – their honour came from their performance, and a perceived superiority to their rivals.

It was later that metallurgy and better design were combined, and British manufacturers began to compete with each other in the specifications of their own engines. The prewar motorcyclist had such variety to choose from; the Matchless Silver Hawk (a narrow-angle V4, all cylinders

contained within a single block), Brough Superior's flat-four Golden Dream, the Square Four Ariel, the straight-four American Ace, and the purring two-strokes of Alfred Scott in Yorkshire.

One of the great truths of motorcycling is that design is self-regulating. Because motorcycles lean over to go round corners, there is a strict limit on almost every aspect of design. Every motorcycle, from humble commuter to out-and-out racing machine, uses the same technology.

The superbike's nearest relative is often the Grand Prix race bike. Thus it was, when motorcycle racing came to be dominated (for more than two decades spanning the war years) by Norton's 500cc single-cylinder racer, which became known as the Manx Norton after the war, that the definitive road superbikes also had one cylinder. Naturally enough, the most desirable of them all was a Norton which shared the racer's engine — detuned to make it more manageable for the road. This was the 500cc Norton International, a long-lived sports road bike with a single overhead camshaft, genuine 100mph-plus top speed, and a fine pedigree.

The Inter sired many imitations, and not all of them had the Norton's credentials. Two in particular achieved a legendary status in spite of having their overhead valves operated by pushrods: the BSA DBD34 Gold Star, and the Velocette Venom. Like the Norton, these were 100mph machines, with deep bellowing exhaust notes and accurate steering and roadholding. Cynics say that these qualities were the result more of very limited suspension movement and not much weight than any particular inspiration of design.

These were not particularly easy motorcycles to live with. Starting the engine, for instance, was a business that demanded a stout heart and an even stouter leg on the kickstart. It is no easy task turning over a big, high-compression piston fast enough to ensure that it will fire up and keep running, and start-up was a carefully orchestrated and timed ritual that included full use of the valve lifter-decompressor lever and manual retardation of the ignition. Even so, many were the ankles strained and calf muscles gouged by a backfiring big single.

In the 1950s the single-cylinder was deposed from automatic racing victory by the Italians, with their four-cylinder machines from Gilera and MV Agusta (not to mention the illustrious though not particularly successful V8 from Moto Guzzi, the most complicated and evocative racer of all time). By now the roadgoing superbike had grown in size from the premier racing size of 500cc, and had diverged.

Again, it was the British manufacturers who led the way. The Triumph Speed Twin (actually a prewar design) set the

pattern for a generation of superbikes: parallel twins with overhead valves (but not overhead camshafts) which rapidly settled on 650cc as the optimum size, and which continued to rule the roost for almost two decades.

The course of development of the Speed Twin is typical. Designed by the legendary Edward Turner, it was introduced as a 500cc model in 1938, and grew to 650cc in 1950. In 1959, the immortal twin-carburettor Bonneville was born (the name was acquired after a Triumph broke the world land speed record at the Bonneville Salt Flats in the USA). The Bonnie was probably the best-known motorcycle of its generation. Ultimately it grew to 750cc, surviving in the process the collapse not only of the original Triumph firm, but also that of the workers' cooperative that succeeded it. Perhaps its finest incarnation was that produced by the Co-op, the 750 Eight-Valve. Despite its qualities the machine was overtaken by circumstances and came to nothing.

The generation of parallel twins had many revered denizens. One was the Norton, which like the Triumph saw its final flowering as a promoted 650 – the Dominator grew into the 850 Commando. This had electric start and a novel way of controlling what was the parallel twin's greatest bugbear, engine vibration. Norton's Isolastic system let the engine shake about, but isolated the rider by rubber-mounting not only the power unit, but also the rest of the power train including the rear pivoted fork.

Among the BSAs, the Royal Enfields, the Matchlesses, AJSs, Triumphs and Nortons of the postwar generation,

there was one British motorcycle that rose above them all. Exclusive and expensive, it was the definitive superbike of its time. The Vincent (the tank badge carried both words) was certainly faster than anything else around and incorporated many design features that were years ahead of its time. One such was the rear suspension, which used a triangulated structure operating springs and dampers located under the seat – a system that predated Yamaha's mono-shock by two decades. But it was the engine that made a legend of the Vincent. It was an all-aluminium over-head-valve Vee-twin of 1000cc with a broad spread of power, and it could lope along relaxedly at 100mph, and gallop to 125mph or more. The Vincent was rather too expensive for its own good, however, and the firm ceased production in 1957.

In the USA, the superbike ethic had gone its own way. By this stage there were only two manufacturers of note left: Indian and Harley Davidson, and the former was soon to perish. This left Harley, who sustained their reputation for robustness without breaking any performance records, and continued to build large-capacity low-revving Vee-twins as if nothing was happening anywhere else.

Through the 1960s, American riders bent on high performance had to rely on imported British bikes, or perhaps (if they were rich and lucky) an MV Agusta, a complex twin-camshaft four-cylinder piece of exotica based closely on the same firm's racing models. Meanwhile Japanese manufacturers were gathering strength, and Honda, Suzuki, Yamaha and the late Bridgestone were showing that 350cc bikes need not necessarily be much slower than 650s.

At the end of the decade the British industry had one last kick at building a superbike – a three-cylinder machine with a 750cc engine and an exhaust note that sent a shiver down your spine. It came in two forms, the Triumph Trident and the BSA Rocket 3. The latter had the engine canted forward. Its racing versions were invincible. However, its specification was old-fashioned, with push-rods operating the overhead valves, and furthermore it was complex to manufacture. In the face of the rising tide of Japanese superbikes, the Tri-dent/Rocket was unable to hold its own, and, having survived from 1969 until 1977, was one of the final casualties of the dying but still complacent British industry.

The Japanese had begun by manufacturing machines in the smaller capacity classes, but in the mid-1960s they served notice that they would not limit themselves for ever. The machine that was the herald of things to come was Honda's CB450, dubbed the Black Bomber, which startled the motorcycling world with more than just its sophisticated engine. It challenged the established order of 650 twins by offering greater performance from a smaller engine. This

was achieved by the engine's capacity to rev way beyond the accepted ceiling of around 6,500rpm, and to top out at a giddy 9,500rpm. The engine design was a racebred twin, and included twin overhead camshafts and ingenious torsion-bar valve springs.

Honda had more to come. In 1969 they introduced the machine that changed the world – the CB750. Four cylinders, four carburettors, four exhaust pipes, and a disc brake – it was a revelation both in terms of design and performance.

Until then, the only modern four-cylinder motorcycle had been the MV Agusta. The Honda was quite different. It was a motorcycle for everyone, the father of the modern super-bike, and it marked the start of the new golden age. At 100mph, with almost 15mph still to go, anyone riding a Honda could afford to laugh at someone trying to keep up on an out-of-breath British 650. Only the Triumph Trident could hope to match it, on a good day. But there were three other Japanese manufacturers with an interest too, and they were not going to take this lying down.

Suzuki gave the first reply, with a machine that was quirky then, and remains so in retrospect. Their empire was founded on buzzing little two-strokes, the largest being a nominal 350cc (actually 315cc). Suzuki's first superbike was also a two-stroke, of a new breed. Three water-cooled cylinders across the frame earned the bike the soubriquet Kettle and purple-and-white paint proclaimed it as something special. Performance was similar to that of the Honda, and the

GT750 was developed into a successful racing machine, campaigned (among others) by Barry Sheene.

Kawasaki were by now a rising force and set out to out-perform these new monsters of the road. They also chose three-cylinder two-strokes, but stayed with air-cooling to keep weight down. Their 500cc Mach III became a legend: erratic roadholding and acceleration so vivid that the blue smoke it left behind might as well have come from the tyres as the three exhausts. This was only the start.

Kawasaki's Mach IV was a 750cc machine based on the same design principles, but even faster. This machine introduced the average road rider to the wheelie: it was almost impossible to *stop* the front wheel lifting off the road as the two-stroke power came on with a snap through the gears.

Honda had not merely led the way, they had started the fashion. Their four-cylinder across-the-frame four-stroke became the standard of the Japanese industry through the 1970s. First to follow were Kawasaki, with the double over-head camshaft Z900 of 1971, which gave rise to a genera-tion of bikes that peaked in air-cooled form with the sport-ing Z1R (or perhaps the later GPz1100, the first motorcycle with fuel injection) and continues to the present day with the liquid-cooled GPz range. Next to follow were Suzuki, whose GS750 and then GS1000 were very similar to the Kawasakis in basic design. However, they started a trend towards integrated styling with their 1100cc Katana of 1981, which has an angular fairing that blends into the fuel tank.

Honda, in the meantime, continued to refine their designs, adding twin overhead camshafts and race-developed chassis components. Probably the finest of their air-cooled fours was the CB1100R, a limited-production 1981 model that was designed with production bike racing in mind. Its standards of braking, roadholding and performance showed how much could be achieved with care, money, and the use of more exotic materials than were practicable in mass production.

Yamaha were the last to join the trend for four-cylinder monsters and they jumped in in a big way. Their XS1100 was the biggest bike yet, when it arrived in 1978, and was subtly different as well as extremely heavy. It used shaft drive in-stead of the ubiquitous chain, and car-style vacuum control for the ignition advance to give a widespread of lazy but plentiful power. More a tourer than a sports bike, the XS1100 was still a gigantic performer, with a top speed approaching 130mph.

While the British industry simply collapsed under this on-slaught, European and American manufacturers regrouped and fought back. In the case of Europe, the tactic was pre-dominantly to continue to do what they were good at – building machines of robust simplicity compared with the

Most exciting of the breed of big Japanese fours were their sporting variants.

RIGHT: Yamaha's XS1100S – a shaft-drive heavyweight with some of the flab removed.

OPPOSITE RIGHT: Kawasaki's Z1R, immortal in more ways than its apparent indestructability.

BELOW: Suzuki's GSX1100 Katana, first of the high-fashion sports road-bikes and now regarded as something of a style classic.

Japanese complexity, achieving comparable performance through light weight and refined roadholding.

The shining example came from Ducati, who designed a smooth and beautiful Vee-twin with exotic desmodromic valve gear (dispensing with springs to close the valves mechanically). It was at first a 750, but grew to 860cc (nominally 900), and later to a full 1000cc. Its finest expression was in the 900SS, a spartan and slender sporting bike of the mid-1970s that introduced many riders to the integrity of race-style roadholding (and the discomfort of race-style suspension).

Still in Italy, Moto Guzzi perfected a range based around a 750cc (later 1000cc) Vee-twin engine that was disposed with the crankshaft lengthways, using shaft drive. The pushrod engine had been designed as a military pump unit, but made a fine motorcycle unit in spite of its pedestrian origins – pumping out massive torque at relatively low rpm. The machines live on.

Italian Batallion — and a grand Dutch oddity.

ABOVE: The Laverda Montjuic was a thinly disguised racer — throaty exhaust, harsh suspension, a high-revving six-speed 500cc twin engine, and an urge for the fast life.

ABOVE RIGHT: Holland's Van Veen OCR was pricey, potent, and very heavy. Premature termination of its Wankel Rotary engine, borrowed from a proposed Citroen car, also killed the bike.

RIGHT: The Ducati 900SS could also switch from road to track with few changes — here the long-legged and stable vee-twin tackles the Isle of Man T T course.

OPPOSITE ABOVE AND BELOW: Italy also produced the first ever six-cylinder superbike. It was a 750cc Benelli, here in a later, more stylish 900cc guise.

Moto Guzzi had been historic stalwarts of motorcycling; Laverda were newcomers, the progeny of an agricultural equipment firm. They also stuck to two cylinders at first, relying on exacting engineering to make the most of their overhead-camshaft designs. Their first superbike was the 1969 750S, but it was the production-racing SFC that made their name — stripped for action, painted a vivid orange, and with a deep-throated bellow from the twin exhausts. The 500cc twin-cam Montjuic of the late-1970s was the natural child of the 750SFC. Laverda's bid for superbike glory was reinforced in the mid-1970s by their big three-cylinder twin-cam range. This was produced in sizes as large as 1200cc, but it is the 1000cc Jota that became a legend, a brutish machine which was raucous, firmly sprung, and very, very fast. MV Agusta, meanwhile, continued to refine their four-cylinder twin-camshaft model, culminating in the glorious 850cc Boxer, beautifully styled and as exotic as ever.

Europe's largest manufacturer was BMW, who throughout the 1970s remained true to their original concept of 1928: a simple pushrod flat twin, crankshaft disposed longitudinally for shaft drive, with the well-cooled cylinders poking into the wind. Refined over the years, this model reached its ultimate in the R100RS of 1976, a 125mph-plus machine of rare quality and beauty. Relatively light, mechanically simple and quiet, the 1000cc RS boasted as its chief distinction a fairing designed in a wind-tunnel to give the best combination yet achieved of streamlining, aerodynamic stability, weather protection and looks. Although it has been replaced by the three- and four-cylinder BMWs,

the R100RS remains a machine of classic elegance.

Not everybody thought that the reciprocating engine was the right answer for the new breed of 1970's superbike. The Wankel Rotary engine held many superficial attractions, especially lightness and compact dimensions. Suzuki were the only Japanese firm to be lured down what turned out to be a blind alley, with a short-lived rotary model – the RE5 – which appeared in 1975.

The European effort was to a much grander scale. It was the Van Veen OCR1000, the first 100-horsepower bike on the road – big, handsome, fast, and very rare. Though the firm was Dutch, the bike was built in Germany, using a French rotary engine intended for use in Citroën cars. The engine project foundered, however, and the bike (born in 1978) died with it in 1980.

More recently, the rotary concept has come alive again as has one famous British marque long considered dead and buried. Norton have revived both the design and their fortunes with a twin rotor engine used for both race and road bikes. After 20 years of development, it was finally launched to the public with the 1987 Commando and later released as a replica of their Formula One bike. This current top of the range model is featured later in the book.

There was one last extravagance of the late 1970s, before superbikes found a new maturity (and new levels of performance) in the 1980s: the six-cylinder monsters. The first of them came from Italy, where automotive industrialist Alessandro de Tomaso had decided to tackle the Japanese head-on. His 127mph Benelli Sei of 1973 was a 750 (later 900) six-cylinder piece of extravagance that set off an excessively wide engine with a splendidly shiny set of six silencers.

It was Honda, in 1978, who brought true technical sophistication to the configuration, maximizing the power of their 1047cc CBX1000 with twin camshafts, while minimizing the width by moving all ancillaries away from the crankshaft ends. The alternator, for example, was mounted behind the bank of cylinders. With 105 horsepower, almost 140mph on tap and a rev ceiling beyond 9,000rpm, the Honda Six had as much technology as anyone had ever seen on a motorcycle. It progressed from a supersports model to become a fully-faired gentleman's express, but was superseded by Honda's (and other people's) four-cylinder models. It was simply too complex for its own good.

In the late 1980s, it looked like the end for the six. Kawasaki's massive feat of engineering, the Z1300, remained on sale until 1987 and the six-cylinder legend seemed in danger of disappearing along with it. Yet in 1988, Honda surprised everybody by releasing a 1500cc version of their Gold Wing luxury tourer powered by a six-cylinder, horizontally-opposed engine. It remains the only six-cylinder machine generally available. Technical complexity for its own sake is now largely a problem of the past in this age of high efficiency. Only the power has gone on increasing.

THE BIKES

BRITAIN

ENGINE
Air and oil-cooled, turbo-
charged, DOHC in-line four

CUBIC CAPACITY:
1052cc

MAXIMUM POWER:
148bhp at 9500rpm

BORE × STROKE:
76 × 58mm

GEARBOX:
five-speed

FINAL DRIVE:
roller chain

WHEELBASE:
1498 to 1574mm (59 to 62in)
variable

DRY WEIGHT:
200kg (440lb)

TOP SPEED:
270kph (170mph)

STANDING QUARTER MILE:
9.8sec

DATE OF LAUNCH:
1989

Imagine a motorcycle capable of covering the standing quarter mile in less than ten seconds, breaking the finishing beams at 155mph; an ultimate street bike.

This Harris Turbo GSX-R1100 is one such. It is not a production motorcycle but a fine example of how a stock Japanese bike engine can be transformed into one of the fastest, most stunning-looking, street legal two-wheelers in the world. It belongs to English enthusiast Ian King who built it and regularly races it in street class drag meetings. He also rides it to work every day.

In no sense is it an ordinary bike. At its heart is a Suzuki GSX-R1100 motor fitted with a Mr Turbo blower kit. It has a single Keihin carb, a fuel pump and a trick Harris exhaust that exits unconventionally out alongside the rear subframe.

The motor has standard GSX-R1100J 1052 pistons but runs a high compression ratio. Given the absence of low-compression pistons, normally found on a turbo conversion, the bottom end has been beefed-up. The pistons ride on Carillo rods and the valve timing has been altered to provide more overlap.

Dissipation of heat is always a problem with turbos and there are two oil coolers, one of which routes oil away from the excessively hot cylinder head. To avoid detonation, the battery box, pressurized from the inlet manifold, doubles as a water reservoir, and injects water into the carb venturi to cool the burn.

The turbo is set to cut in at 3000rpm and, with boost pressure anywhere between 15 and 30psi, top speed is somewhere over the rainbow. The bike is geared for a theoretical 175mph. In truth, Ian doesn't know how fast it will go but he has an awful lot of fun trying to find out.

The beautiful alloy perimeter beam frame and curved, single-sided swingarm were made by Harris Performance, a small specialist chassis firm whose main interest is in racing and frame/suspension development. They reckon the frame and swingarm assembly is the most rigid they've ever built. The swingarm was inspired by Honda's RC30 but uses completely different suspension linkages. It sports an RC30 stub axle and eccentric adjustors which allows Ian to adjust the wheelbase making it either short for road use or at full extension for the drag strip allowing maximum traction. The swingarm also doubles as an air reservoir for the gearbox airshifter.

As you'd expect, the cycle parts are top quality. All the brackets, yokes, footrests and plates were made by Harris. The wheels are super-light magnesium alloy Dymags, 17-inchers front and rear. The inverted front forks are by White Power. The rear suspension is by an Ohlins Formula-One spec shock. The brakes are a hotch-potch of superlative components. The 320mm fully-floating front discs are made by Spondon and gripped by four-piston ISR calipers. The rear disc is from an RC30 with a Lockheed caliper. The front brake and hydraulic clutch both use Brembo radial Goldline master cylinders and share the same fluid reservoir. Goodridge braided steel, aircraft-quality hosing is used for the brake, clutch and numerous oil lines.

Perhaps more important than this expensive shopping list of cycle parts is the way it's all been put together. Ian reckons he spent 200 hours building the bike and the neat, compact layout of every sub-assembly makes everything quickly accessible. Every component from the merest bracket or plate is perfectly finished. It's not just attention to detail but sheer engineering artistry.

Ian refuses to reveal how much the bike cost to build so let's just say you could probably buy three standard GSX-R1100s for the cost of one Ian King turbo special. Consider the cosmetic touches alone – the modified OWO1 Harris fairing, the custom-made seat and tank, the shimmering Mirage paintwork – and so it's no surprise to learn this bike has won numerous show awards for its elegance, and for its engineering.

Wherever it goes, Ian King's bike turns heads and attracts admirers. It is one of Britain's most exciting and radical bikes yet, beyond its stunning looks there lies a serious and professionally built motorcycle. Only its owner knows what it's like to sail across the drag strip finishing line at over 150mph having run the quarter mile from a standing start in 9.8 seconds. He says it is pure magic.

NORTON F1

BRITAIN

ENGINE:
Liquid-cooled, twin chamber
rotary

CUBIC CAPACITY:
588cc nominal

MAXIMUM POWER:
94bhp at 9500rpm

BORE × STROKE:
not applicable
(compression ratio 9:1)

GEARBOX:
five-speed

WHEELBASE:
1440mm (56.7in)

FINAL DRIVE:
roller chain

DRY WEIGHT:
192kg (423lb)

TOP SPEED:
248kph (155mph)

STANDING QUARTER MILE:
11.5sec

DATE OF LAUNCH:
1989

Nobody could accuse Norton Motors of rushing the rotary into production. Prototypes were first shown to the press in the 1970s. By 1985, the bike had still not gone into production but it was being steadily developed and was in use with several British police forces who reported on it favourably. It wasn't until 1987 that a civilian model rotary, the Commander, appeared. That same year Norton returned to the world's racetracks with the RCW588, a potent, hand-built race bike that was difficult to place in top flight competition because of arguments about its capacity – was it a 600 or a 1200? By 1988, Norton had attracted considerable sponsorship from John Player and although the racer did little on the World Formula-One stage, it easily won the British Formula-One Championship. It was a success not lost on Norton's marketing department who widely publicized the victory even in the non-motorcycle press.

To a home audience starved of seeing a British bike factory in competition, the racing Nortons are a crowd puller. Though they've yet to win on the Isle of Man, on any other British track they usually start favourite.

The Norton F1 is a rolling tribute to the race bike's success. Although it, too, is hand-built and a strictly limited edition, the F1 is not really a race replica just a very fine sports bike for the roads.

The twin rotor engine has been turned through 180-degrees compared to the racer, because the F1 carries a Yamaha FZR1000 gear-cluster inside its Norton gear-case. Reversing the engine position has had advantages in terms of compactness, better air flow and shorter inlet tracts.

Like all rotary engines, the unit is free-revving and smooth. It combines tremendous flexibility as well as an impressive turn of speed. The engine's prime asset is its wide range of power, together with an ability to rev freely without vibration or strain. Both its performance and the noise it makes are unique. With three firing strokes per revolution, the rotary has hallmarks of both the two-stroke (in simplicity, lightness and lack of engine braking) and the four-stroke (torque and power spread). It's so smooth it needs a rev limiter at 10,500rpm. In top gear at maximum wick, its 94hp carries it to a top speed of close to 150mph. In contrast, the factory racer produces 140hp and has been timed at 189mph.

The two bikes are closer in specification when it comes to the rolling chassis. Both bikes have hand-crafted Spondon twin-spar aluminium frames. The F1 is expensively equipped with state-of-the art White Power suspension – inverted forks and a single shock, rising rate rear. Both ends are multi-adjustable and true to Norton's tradition, the bike has excellent steering, suspension and roadholding. To scrub off

OPPOSITE ABOVE: The Norton F-One replica, a hand-built 94hp road bike weighing 192kg with a top speed of 155mph.

OPPOSITE BELOW: The real F-One racer on which it was based. The RCW588, here seen in the hands of factory rider Trevor Nation, is a 140hp works missile weighing 145kg with a top speed of 190mph.

the speed, they fitted excellent Brembo full floating discs grabbed by four-piston opposed calipers. The tyres are Michelin with a really fat 170/60 rear. For stable road use, the wheelbase is a lengthy 56.7in. Even with the burden of roadster running gear like lights and starter motor, the dry weight is only 423lb. Overall the bike's dimensions are closer to that of a 500cc GP two-stroke than the 750 thumpers its racing relation regularly competes against.

Norton built a first batch of 200 F1's that were eagerly snapped up; sales included a large order from eager buyers in Japan. Another batch of 200 is now planned and the factory are hoping thereby to homologate the bike for World Superbike competition in 1991.

The F1 with its snug fitting, fully enclosed bodywork, stark black lines and striking graphics won a prestigious British Styling Agency design award in 1989 for styling agency Seymour Powell.

That the F1 exists at all is a fitting tribute to the survival and resurrection of a great British bike factory. The rotary always was the project that was meant to survive long after the original production lines had ceased. That they are now back in serious production with one of the finest sports bikes in the world is heartening. Quite simply, the Norton F1 is the finest British motorcycle ever made.

SPONDON SUZUKI 1260

There is more to this bike than meets the eye. Much more. English enthusiast Steve Burns wanted to create the ultimate special using his own engineering ability and the talents of experts where appropriate. He fitted only the best cycle parts available, assembling and moulding the individual components into the fastest, best handling, most visually stunning street bike around. 'All my knowledge and ideas from years of building bikes went into this one' says Steve. The rolling result speaks for itself. If there is strength in numbers, consider that the V&M tuned engine makes 174bhp at 10,500rpm and 107ft/lb of torque at 7000rpm. Or how about the bike having been electronically timed at 183mph?

The incredibly strong motor started life as a GSX-R1100, the older 1052cc model. At V&M Racing, a tuning shop whose proprietor Jack Valentine is a European Pro-Stock drag racing champion, the standard production engine was transformed from a humble mass-manufactured unit producing 115bhp into a very special hand-built 1260cc motor with 174hp on tap. That is more outright horsepower than any other motorcycle in this book. More even than the factory 500cc GP racers.

The 1260 conversion involves boring out the crankcases to accommodate new liners. The 1260 Pro Series Wiseco pistons have short skirts and hand-machined tops but they're still relatively heavy so ride on extra strong and reliable Carillo connecting rods. Compression is 12:1. All the magic, according to Jack Valentine, is in matching the cylinder head to the chosen cam. Here the head has been gas-flowed and meticulously ported, polished and finished. The cams are hard-welded and reprofiled to full race specification. It runs standard valve sizes but each of the 16 valves are hand-finished and assembled in the head with heavy-duty springs. The gas is fed by a bank of Mikuni 38mm flat slide smoothbores, expensive but ultra-efficient at improving top end power and boosting throttle response. The exhaust system is an American Eagle Formula-One stainless steel four-into-two-into-one pipe with big diameter header pipes and a pretty illegal silencer. The ignition is a Vance and Hines drag racing unit, as is the heavy-duty clutch. Steve designed and built a secondary oil cooling system just to pump more oil to the cylinder head. The radiator for this system is neatly located under the seat, hence the vents in the ducktail.

To cope with the horsepower the frame needed to be of equally Herculean properties. The specialist English chassis firm, Spondon Engineering, designed a double box-section using extruded aluminium beam frame (7020 Series) which is highly-polished and very rigid. Suspension is by inverted

White Power front forks and a rising-rate Ohlins rear shock. The floating brake discs and four-piston calipers are made by Spondon using ISR master cylinders. The wheels are 17in (front) and 18in (rear) made by Marvic. The fairing and seat unit are much-modified Harris items while Steve fashioned the six gallon tank himself. Dream Machine did all the understated paintwork.

It is most definitely an ultimate streetbike. Steve has won numerous drag races on this machine running the quarter mile in 10 seconds dead. A true enthusiast and quite a character, Steve likes nothing better than to cover the quarter mile pulling monster wheelies with the bike vertical on its back wheel and the front wheel reaching for the sky. It is not a talent for the faint-hearted and requires enormous skill in throttle control and balance. On numerous occasions he has overdone it and unloaded at high speed. Such exploits have earnt him various nicknames like 'Flipper', 'Showboat' and the perennial favourite – Steve 'Friction' Burns. To prove he was the fastest wheelie merchant around, Steve organized an observed World Record run on this bike at Bruntingthorpe Proving Ground. The result is in the *Guinness Book of Records* – World's Fastest Wheelie – Steve Burns (Spondon Suzuki 1260) – 151mph.

GERMANY

ENGINE:
Liquid-cooled, DOHC, in-line
horizontal four

CUBIC CAPACITY:
987cc

MAXIMUM POWER:
100bhp at 8000rpm

BORE × STROKE:
67 × 70mm

GEARBOX:
five-speed

FINAL DRIVE:
shaft

WHEELBASE:
1565mm (61.6in)

DRY WEIGHT:
245kg (540lb)

TOP SPEED:
238kph (149mph)

STANDING QUARTER MILE:
11.5sec

DATE OF LAUNCH:
1989

The BMW K1 was the solution to a serious problem that faced Europe's largest motorcycle manufacturer in the late 1980s. Although well-established the product line-up was looking increasingly tired and dated. Their range of K100, K75 and flat-twin touring roadsters enjoyed a solid reputation for quality engineering and reliability. However, the market was experiencing unprecedented demand for large capacity sports bikes. In comparison to the sports flagships of the Japanese, BMW's bikes appeared tame and a touch staid. The company needed a new pure sports motorcycle. In 1989, they unveiled the K1, and what a striking, sensational-looking motorcycle it was.

Designed to attract big sports bike enthusiasts and to keep BMW alive in the fiercest of markets, the K1 has succeeded on all fronts largely because it *is* so different.

The bike's distinctive bodywork, including the virtually-enclosed front wheel and bulbous tail section, is designed to make it aerodynamically efficient. Viewed head on, the bike presents a huge frontal area but this tapers away to the rear tail hump and gives an impressive drag coefficient of .38, a figure better than any other currently produced motorcycle. Its slippery shape helps it maintain a top speed in comfort for the rider, who is well-protected from the wind-rush.

BMW needed an aerodynamic advantage because, in Germany motorcycle horsepower output is limited to a maximum of 100bhp. The 1984, four cylinder K100 engine was extensively revised, doubling the number of valves to 16, reworking the combustion chambers and lightening the crankshaft, con rods and pistons, so the unit revved harder. Perhaps the most important change was the adoption of the Bosch Motronic digital engine management system as fitted to BMW cars. This combines control of the fuel injection and ignition systems giving enhanced response, ample power and good fuel economy.

To match their new genuine 100hp engine, BMW built a fine rolling chassis. The frame is uprated from the K100 series in that, although the engine still forms part of the frame with the single rear suspension arm pivoting on the casings, the frame tubing is in larger diameter tubing and the bike has a longer wheelbase and shorter trail. The paralever single-sided arm is articulated to avoid driveshaft torque reaction.

For front suspension and brakes, BMW fitted some expensive Italian components. The large diameter front forks are made by Marzocchi. The brakes – large 305mm floating discs gripped by four-piston calipers – are by Brembo. In addition, the bike comes with BMW's own, exclusive ABS or anti-lock braking system. Electronic sensors monitor the

OPPOSITE: **BMW's striking K1 looks like no other production motorcycle. Its huge frontal area and aerodynamically efficient bodywork really work for the rider at speed allowing day-long cruising in comfort at well over 100mph.**

comparative speed of front and rear wheels and releases brake pressure up to seven times a second, preventing possible lock up of the wheels. The ABS system is a boon to road safety and BMW are still the only manufacturer to have put ABS into production. It's been an option on all their big bikes since 1988.

Using the widest wheels ever fitted to a BMW, the K1 responds to being ridden aggressively. Despite an enormous wet weight of 570lb, the bike is surprisingly nimble and easy to ride. Its forte is the wide open, fast road where its effortless maximum speed can be fully exploited.

It remains a special kind of motorcycle. Originally only 2,500 were to be built but worldwide demand means the production figure is likely to be revised. The K1 is the only BMW ever built that's unable to carry hard panniers (the swoopy tail section prevents fitment though BMW do offer a soft luggage system that occupies the pillion seat making the K1 a true solo sportster). In response to demand from their traditional touring customers, in 1990 BMW released a 16-valve version of the K100RS. This bike can carry hard panniers. Apart from bodywork and styling, its specification is virtually identical to the K1 even though it looks nothing like it. As a modern superbike, the K1 stands alone – proud, defiant and *very* different.

GERMANY

ENGINE:
Opposed twin, OHV four/valve

CUBIC CAPACITY:
980cc

MAXIMUM POWER:
80bhp at 6250rpm

BORE × STROKE:
94 × 70.6mm

GEARBOX:
five-speed

FINAL DRIVE:
cardan shaft, crown-wheel-and-pinion

WHEELBASE:
1380mm (54.4in)

DRY WEIGHT:
197kg (435lb)

TOP SPEED:
222kph (139mph)

STANDING QUARTER MILE:
12.3sec

DATE OF LAUNCH:
1982

There will always be a small number of motorcycle enthusiasts who insist on something different; it is their aim to improve upon excellence. If the prime mover is a German, he will usually pick on his native BMW as a candidate for the treatment. So it was with Mike Krauser, his name already famous for high quality, quickly detachable luggage systems. He looked at the top BMW of the time, the sporting R100RS, and found it wanting.

First thing to go was the frame. Comfortable suspension and plenty of room for two had no place on the super-sporting machine he envisaged; nor did the simple (and inevitably flexible) tubular frame. Krauser commissioned German aircraft engineers to design an alternative, and they came up with a masterpiece of complexity, a veritable bird-cage of short, straight tubes that double- and triple-triangulated one another for maximum rigidity.

The BMW suspension was modified to eliminate the mid-corner wallows, then the whole was clothed in compact bodywork that echoed the BMW's austere styling without the bulk; the petrol tank, seat and rear mudguard were unified in one piece of glass fibre.

Krauser then turned to the flat-twin engine. The overall design was excellent, well-balanced and well-cooled, but he wanted more flexibility as well as more urge at high revs. He commissioned a more modern four-valve head to replace the BMW's two valves, which not only improved the breathing throughout the rev range, but also lifted the rev ceiling.

The MKM1000 was a long time in the making, and all the careful development work has produced a fine bike. To ride, it is essentially a BMW – the familiar Boxer engine and the sensations of the shaft drive see to that. But it is a BMW apart.

First, there is the riding position, crouched over the bars in a sporting style. It throws the weight forward rather uncomfortably at lower speeds, but the more the wind lifts the rider, the better control becomes. The handling is concomitantly sporting, with a far more direct response to the subtleties of control than any standard BMW.

Engine modifications perform the same function of tautening up the German luxury bike to release its sporting potential. Curiously, the first sensation of the four-valve engine is of milder manners, since the Krauser pulls smoothly and strongly from below 3,000rpm. It is the crispness higher up the rev range that makes it a 130mph-plus machine.

The MKM1000 is exotic, very expensive, and very rare – a special version of a rather special breed.

BELOW AND INSET: The Krauser-BMW MKM 1000 is one man's dream brought to reality. A frame built by the Messerschmidt aero-engineers gives unprecedented levels of sporting roadholding to the versatile BMW flat twin engine, while an eight-valve head releases extra power to match. A rare experience, on road or race-track. Note the one-piece bodywork. The MKM1000 is exotic, very expensive and very rare — a special version of a rather special breed. Although Krauser still make four-valve head conversions for BMW boxers, a bolt-on method of adding 12hp, increasing power by 20 percent on recent 1000cc twins, production of the MKM1000 specials ended in 1989. The production run was 300 and the last 30 were bought by customers in Japan. The new Krauser flagship is the Domani, a BMW K1-powered, hub-centred steered three-wheeler which is neither a sidecar nor a three-wheeled sports car, but more of a new motorcycle-based leisure vehicle of enormous potential.

BMW R100GS

GERMANY

ENGINE:
air-cooled, OHV, horizontally
opposed twin

CUBIC CAPACITY:
980cc

MAXIMUM POWER:
60bhp at 9500rpm

BORE × STROKE:
94 × 70.6mm

GEARBOX:
five-speed, constant mesh

FINAL DRIVE:
shaft and crown-and-wheel-
and-pinion

WHEELBASE:
1513mm (59.6in)

DRY WEIGHT:
206kg (454lb)

TOP SPEED:
184kph (115mph)

STANDING QUARTER MILE:
13.7sec

DATE OF LAUNCH:
1987

The R100GS earns its place in this collection by being one of the world's biggest and fastest off-road bikes. It is *very* good on the road but not so good on the dirt. The GS stands for Geländestrasse or street scrambler. BMW call it 'a hobby bike, a two-wheeled Range Rover' and the comparison is appropriate. It is not a serious dirt bike but it is one of the best all-purpose bikes ever built. Suitably beefed-up factory versions have won the gruelling Paris to Dakar rally on three occasions. In stock production form, the 100GS has proved a popular choice for riders exploring the world on long distance trips across continents with all types of terrain. It is a 115mph road bike that can cope with the rough stuff. The machine is an imaginative mix of parts that were already available on other BMW bikes, spiced with some adventurous engineering. An example is BMW's patented Paralever rear suspension, a one sided swing-arm with a single gas shock unit. In effect, it is half a swing-arm, but BMW's engineers made it both lighter *and* 50 per cent stronger than a conventional assembly. The rear wheel is held on by three bolts, there is nothing you could call an axle. The wheel bearing is big, the crown wheel housing is internally stressed since it has to carry the full loads of the back wheel with 7in of travel available. The Paralever rear suspension works admirably, eliminating driveshaft torque reaction. Quick wheel changing is obviously a bonus.

The front suspension consists of leading axle forks offering a luxurious 8.8in of travel. The bike is tall and needs to be for reasonable ground clearance (8.58in). The steering is quick and the throttle response lively. The whole machine is light and nimble with plenty of power and very good brakes. Like all flat twin BMWs, it has a low centre of gravity, so the bike can be chucked around with abandon. The dual-purpose, knobbly tyres are high-speed rated and tubeless thanks to an innovative cross-spoke wire wheel and isolated rim design. The engine is an updated variant of the R80 road bike endowed with typical BMW performance – bags of torque and a wide spread of power – plus some dual-purpose innovations. The bike has a lightweight clutch and flywheel for quicker throttle response, and low gearing; necessary for a dirt bike but lots of fun anywhere since it helps the GS to wheelie easily. On the open road it will hold 110mph for as long as the rider can face sitting up so high and exposed against the wind. Unfortunately what makes it good on the tarmac tells against it on the dirt. The bike is just *too* big and *too* powerful. Fully gassed (5.7gal) it weighs 454lb, fine for a road bike but a little heavy for serious off-road use. In addition there is the long wheelbase, the unsprung weight of the driveshaft and two horizontal cylinders

OPPOSITE: A Range Rover on two wheels – the BMW gives the smart set the facility for off road riding yet is a sensationally good street or city bike. At better than 100mph flat out, it is far faster than more specialized off road bikes, though it pays a penalty in the weight of its 980cc engine. On a long dirt road with a good surface, there is nothing to touch the Bee-Em – its comfort and road manners are a bonus.

that stick out a long way, all factors that conspire against its dirt ability. These are not problems when traction is positive on firm ground but in mud and real rough stuff, the bike bogs down far too easily.

The R100GS is best used as a cross-country bike, sticking mainly to proper roads but taking the odd short cut and back road where necessary. Above all else, the bike is a lot of fun to ride; it is a functional, practical, rugged and reliable all-rounder. Recently, various BMW importers have released Paris-Dakar replica versions of the bike as a tribute to one of the world's most successful desert racers.

BIMOTA BELLARIA

ITALY

ENGINE:
Liquid-cooled, DOHC, in-line four

CUBIC CAPACITY:
599cc

MAXIMUM POWER:
95bhp at 10,500rpm

BORE × STROKE:
59 × 54.8mm

GEARBOX:
six-speed

FINAL DRIVE:
roller chain

WHEELBASE:
1375mm (54.2in)

DRY WEIGHT:
165kg (364lb)

TOP SPEED:
240kph (150mph)

STANDING QUARTER MILE:
11sec

DATE OF LAUNCH:
1990

bimota

Bimota have the distinction of making the world's most expensive motorcycles. They are handmade creations using all the very best components. Production is labour-intensive, but they are beautifully finished and very fast. Bimota make exclusive, expensive, luxurious sports bikes that approach perfection, that ideal but elusive marriage between horsepower and a frame that can deliver the goods. Take one large Japanese power-plant and place it in a unique frame with the best suspension, wheels and brakes that money can buy.

Bimota's Bellaria is the only Bimota ever designed to carry a dual seat, all their other bikes being strictly solo machines. Typically, though, it sports the distinctive, and very rigid, twin spar aluminium perimeter frame, the highly-finished, fully-integrated bodywork and Italian designer-styling that has become the small Rimini factory's hallmark.

Based around Yamaha's FZR600 engine, comparisons between the stock Japanese bike (itself an acclaimed, best in class model) and the Bimota transformation are instructive. The standard bike weighs 179kg and makes 85hp while the Bellaria scales just 165kg and produces 95hp.

It feels and rides more like a 250 than a middleweight. Bimota build into their bikes a balance, stability and responsiveness that has no peer in modern motorcycle production and the Bellaria is a fine example of their art. With its tight wheelbase and low weight, it steers and handles crisply. The Marzocchi suspension with upside-down forks and a centrally-mounted rear shock offers a firm, well-damped action. The bike has a sharp, rigid feel and is at its best being ridden hard, to the very edge of its fat tyres. High-speed handling is a treat.

The extra 10hp released from Yamaha's highly-respectable and potent FZR 600 engine was found by modifications to the intake system and the fitting of a less restrictive exhaust pipe. Even the styling is integrated to suit the engine tuner's task. The body mouldings channel air along the side of the tank and feed it to the hungry downdraft carbs. Nothing could be done about the Yamaha's clunky gearbox and driveline slop though. At low speeds, the motor snatches at the chain and the transmission is notchy with the occasional false neutral. Naturally the problem disappears at speed and the Bellaria is not the sort of bike where you spend much time dragging the chain.

Its slim lines are perfectly complemented by its simple, elegant styling where paint, plastic and alloy are cleverly matched to enhance the subtle overall impression.

Only 160 examples of this sumptuous looking motorcycle have been produced by the factory where total output is only 1000 bikes a year. For the same price as one Bimota Bellaria you could buy three Yamaha FZR600s but that is hardly the point, is it?

OPPOSITE: The Bellaria, based around Yamaha's FZR600 engine, is one of the smallest motorcycles Bimota have ever made. It's also arguably one of the most beautiful. Sharp handling with more power and less weight than the Yamaha, its performance edge is more than cosmetic though.

BIMOTA YB4

ITALY

ENGINE:
Liquid-cooled, DOHC, in-line
four

CUBIC CAPACITY:
749cc

MAXIMUM POWER:
121bhp at 10,500rpm

BORE × STROKE:
68 × 51.6mm

GEARBOX:
six-speed

FINAL DRIVE:
roller chain

WHEELBASE:
1420mm (55.9in)

DRY WEIGHT:
180kg (397lb)

TOP SPEED:
256kph (160mph)

STANDING QUARTER MILE:
11.7sec

DATE OF LAUNCH:
1988

bimota

In race trim, this motorcycle won the 1987 Formula-One World Championship and ended five years of Honda domination in the most important four-stroke racing class. It was a victory that marked the arrival of Bimota on the world stage. The tiny Italian factory had taken on the mighty Japanese works teams and beaten them fair and square.

Originally the YB4 was a pure racer unavailable for road use. With the advent of the World Superbike Championship in 1988 and its strict homologation rules, Bimota were obliged to build 200 YB4s in order to compete. Inevitably some ended up on the street. They also took the opportunity to make one important change – their Formula-One racer had been normally carburated, but the YB4 that finally went into series production was fuel-injected.

The YB4 has always used a Yamaha FZ750 engine, the pioneering five valve, steeply inclined unit launched in 1985. The standard FZ engine never lacked top end power but was weak in midrange and low down output. It takes some winding up. Bimota's aim was to boost performance through fuel injection. The Weber Marelli electronic system in concert with the ignition advance timing meters the optimum amount of fuel and air through an injector into the intake manifold, to produce the ideal charge at a given rpm. There are sensors to measure the throttle opening, phase of the engine, coolant and air temperature, and air pressure is regulated at a constant three bars. Ignition modules adjust the coil charge, and the whole system is managed by a black box which has an interchangeable chip. In theory, unburnt gases are minimized and fuel consumption reduced. As the engine is being fed the ideal mixture, power is increased across the rev range.

Although very fast in a straight line, it is not power that gives the Bimota its main advantage, rather it is power-to-weight and a beautifully crafted chassis keeps that weight low. The YB4's dry weight is a keen 180kg. The engine is used as a stressed member held in place by massive aluminium beams with huge castings supporting the critical areas around the steering head and rear swingarm pivot. Bimota pioneered aluminium perimeter frame development at a time when all the other manufacturers were still using steel double cradles and their original ideas on how to house heavy Japanese engines have been shamelessly copied. Today, perimeter frames are commonplace.

The YB4 has totally neutral handling – its behaviour is predictable, smooth and supremely forgiving. The steering is sharp and responsive, the suspension stiff and expertly damped. Its quick steering and short wheelbase allow it to change direction very rapidly, yet its handling is never nervous, it feels solid, low and compact, always letting the rider know exactly what the tyres are doing.

Such was Bimota's success with this bike during its heyday of 1987–1989, Yamaha were forced to release their own World Superbike contender, the OWO1, featuring a comprehensively revised FZR750 engine, larger bored, shorter stroking and making appreciably more power than the five-year-old FZ750 design. Because of the homologation rules though, Bimota would have to build another 200 bikes in order to use the new engine. Fuel injecting the older engine has helped increase the power but really it is Bimota's wonderful rolling chassis that keeps the YB4 on the pace and in the hunt. It is a complete, perfectly balanced motorcycle. Racers say that riding it almost becomes an extension of the will, so direct is the feeling of contact with the track surface. All you need is the will to win, and this gorgeous looking motorcycle does the rest.

BIMOTA TUATARA

ITALY

ENGINE:
Liquid-cooled, DOHC, in-line four

CUBIC CAPACITY:
989cc

MAXIMUM POWER:
152bhp at 9500rpm

BORE × STROKE:
75 × 56mm

GEARBOX:
five-speed

FINAL DRIVE:
roller chain

WHEELBASE:
1420mm (56in)

DRY WEIGHT:
168kg (370lb)

TOP SPEED:
280kph (175mph)

STANDING QUARTER MILE:
10.7sec

DATE OF LAUNCH:
1990

Bimota's Tuatara is easily the most expensive and exclusive production motorcycle in this book. It's also arguably the fastest. Production at the small Bimota factory in Rimini was limited to just 60 examples. These were built in response to customer demand for a bike with performance 'superior to a World Superbike racer.' Bimota already had a stable of pretty quick and rare machinery to choose from – like the YB4 racer that had won the 1987 Formula-One World Championship and is easily capable of 160mph plus. Then there was the YB8, a Yamaha FZR1000 Exup-based street bike, normally carburated, making 149hp and 170mph. But no, these rich customers wanted something more, something faster still. Bimota looked at their dyno figures and concluded it was possible. They would build 60 ultimate road bikes selling them at a price befitting their exclusive status.

They chose as a suitable powertrain for the world's fastest motorcycle Yamaha's original FZR1000 – the 989cc unit that preceded the increased bore FZR1000 Exup version of 1003cc. Remarkably, Bimota did little to liberate a big increase in horsepower from the stock engine. They merely fuel-injected it, and fitted their own less restrictive and lightweight stainless steel exhaust. By concentrating solely on efficient induction and exhaust scavenging, Bimota's engine tuners were rewarded with a peak of 152hp at 9500rpm. The motor's top end grunt was simply enormous.

Meanwhile the chassis engineers worked wonders in wedging a large engine into a frame and running gear no larger than that used on a 600cc bike. Indeed, the 1000cc Tuatara weighs only 3kg more than Bimota's 600cc Bellaria. The weight saving exercise begins with a twin-spar aluminium frame, and continues with lightened inverted Marzocchi forks hand-laid carbon-fibre and fibreglass bodywork right through to the magnesium alloy wheels. To save weight around the steering head they replaced the traditional instrument cluster with a slim, electronic digital panel. The wheelbase is a tight 56in. The power-to-weight ratio is as keen as anything on two wheels, racers included.

Beautifully finished and styled and well up to Bimota's usual high standards of quality, the story goes that the factory test rider, Giancarlo Falappa, took the bike speed testing along a deserted Bologna-Ancona motorway at 5am one bright morning. On perfect gearing and after some fine-tuning of the fuel injection system, the factory bike was timed at 300kph or 187mph – which makes it the fastest production road bike in the world – bar none. Attempts to duplicate that speed on the few models made available for testing have proved impossible. Although all 60 Tuataras made were hand-assembled, the factory bike does seem to

OPPOSITE, ABOVE AND BELOW: The most expensive production motorcycle in the world, Bimota's Tuatara has a claimed top speed of 300kph/187mph. Only 60 examples were ever made. The detail shot shows the massive, fully-floating front brake discs.

BELOW, FAR RIGHT: The Tuatara being speed-tested against Kawasaki's ZZR1100.

have been a bit special. A top speed of 175mph appears nearer the mark for the 60 that were released.

At 175 or 187mph there's no denying the Tuatara is in-decently quick. It gets its name from an exotic greenish-grey lizard found only on small islands around New Zealand. They have been around for 225 million years, when the pace of life was definitely a little slower.

ITALY

ENGINE:
Water-cooled, SOHC,
desmodromic, 90-degree,
vee-twin

CUBIC CAPACITY:
904cc

MAXIMUM POWER:
84bhp at 8400rpm

BORE × STROKE:
92 × 68mm

GEARBOX:
six-speed

FINAL DRIVE:
roller chain

WHEELBASE:
1450mm (57.1in)

DRY WEIGHT:
205kg (452lb)

TOP SPEED:
220kph (138mph)

STANDING QUARTER MILE:
12sec

DATE OF LAUNCH:
1988

The Paso 906 was a significant bike for Ducati, their first to really aim at a slice of the mass market dominated by the Japanese. Although firmly committed to the merits of a vee-twin, Ducati realized that the days of their air-cooled, two valve, desmo unit hung in a lean sporting chassis were strictly numbered. They needed more power and efficiency, and they also needed to pass increasingly stringent emission controls. Their old bikes were too noisy. Worse still their exhausts pumped an awful lot of damaging hydrocarbons out into the atmosphere. Ducati needed to clean up and refine their act, attracting new customers while hopefully not alienating traditional Ducati enthusiasts. The Paso 906 was their answer to this challenge and is in many ways a transitional offering between the fabled Dukes of old (like the 750 and 900SS) and the truly fabulous bikes yet to come (like the 851 superbike).

Although it looked like a million dollars, the 906 Paso received a fairly cool reception from road testers and buyers alike. It was too different from the old Ducatis to attract the cognoscenti (or *Ducatisti*), yet it wasn't different or fast enough to attract buyers of big Japanese sports bikes. It was certainly a brave move on Ducati's part, but it didn't quite come off. With the benefit of hindsight, it's easy to see now that it was a convenient halfway house, a bold step between Ducati's past and future. In the language of the market though, the Paso looked better than it cooked.

Designed by the then technical director, Dr Massimo Bordi, the 906 engine is actually 904cc (the factory obviously didn't feel that 904 Paso had the right ring to it). It was a new engine, sharing some of the development that would later be seen on the 851 – both have the same slim crankcases, six-speed gearbox and dry clutch. But whereas the 851 would carry twin cams and four valve heads, the Paso was stuck with a traditional Ducati valve-train – a single cam and two valves, desmo operated of course.

The new engine was water-cooled and incredibly oversquare, the 92mm pistons being much larger than anything Ducati had previously fitted. Fed by a big twin-choke 44mm Weber carb, the engine made good power with lots of torque and a new-found appetite for high revs. The carburation and ignition seemed particularly well-sorted. Between 3000 and the 9000rpm redline, there were no flat spots or huge steps, just straight up, linear power. About the worst aspect of the new motor was its lack of noise. The water-cooling handily absorbed any mechanical clutter but the new exhaust system restricted the distinctive vee-twin rumble to a muffle and doubtless stifled some of its low-down power too.

OPPOSITE: Ducati's 906 Paso was a transitional bike between the single cam, two valve Dukes of old and the DOHC, four valve 851 superbikes yet to come. It was innovative in being water-cooled and wearing powerfully-styled, fully-integrated bodywork but its over-tyred, small wheels made the handling disappointing. For 1991, Ducati unveiled a bigger-wheeled, fuel-injected version with more power.

The box section steel frame, the Marzocchi/Ohlins suspension and Brembo brakes performed in the time-honoured Ducati fashion, giving redoubtable handling and a stiff, taut ride. They made a mistake in fitting 16in wheels front and back though. The fashion for quick steering 16in front wheels had stemmed from the 500cc GP bikes of the mid-1980s, but had been superseded by the development and undeniable all-round merit of 17in wheels long before Ducati unveiled the Paso Arguably overtyred with a 130/60-16 front radial, the steering needs to be firmly wrestled with to prevent understeer and the bike tends to stand upright if braked when heeled over In its favour, the steering response and front wheel behaviour becomes quicker, predictable and more acceptable the faster you go. But then there's the problem of the riding position, which is not exactly comfortable or adaptable and has most riders looking down on the bike unable to fully tuck in behind the low screen.

The lovely, fully integrated bodywork created by Italian craftsman, Massimo Tamburini and finished in traditional fire-engine red, gives the bike forceful visual impact. But for too many die-hard Ducati enthusiasts, the Paso lacked character. It may have looked like *La Dolce Vita* on two wheels but really it was a harbinger of greater and more potent motorbikes yet to come.

ITALY

ENGINE:
Liquid-cooled, DOHC, 90-
degree, vee-twin

CUBIC CAPACITY:
851cc

MAXIMUM POWER:
105bhp at 9000rpm

BORE × STROKE:
92 × 64mm

GEARBOX:
six-speed

FINAL DRIVE:
roller chain

WHEELBASE:
1430mm (56.3in)

DRY WEIGHT:
181kg (398lb)

TOP SPEED:
243kph (152mph)

STANDING QUARTER MILE:
11.2sec

DATE OF LAUNCH:
1989

This is an astonishing and beautiful motorcycle. It's the fastest production four-stroke vee-twin in the world. It's also the only twin cylinder motorcycle capable of holding its own in World Championship Superbike racing. It can not only run with the best 750cc four-cylinder racers built, it can beat them.

In engine configuration, Ducati's 851 pays tribute to traditional classic design – a 90-degree vee-twin in perfect primary balance with desmodromic valve operation so that the valves are opened and shut mechanically rather than by springs. Yet it is also a modern masterpiece – dual overhead camshafts, four valves per cylinder and complicated, fully programmable, Weber fuel injection. Add a racing-spec, rolling chassis, some truly inspired Italian styling and paint the whole bike in bright racing red and you have a sports sensation, a two-wheeled dream machine – expensive, rare and very fast.

The 851 comes in various forms, from road bike to production racer to full blown factory superbike, and its worldwide success has largely revived Ducati's fortunes as a manufacturer. Designed by Ducati's legendary Chief Engineer, Fabio Taglioni, and completed by his successor, Massimo Bordi, the 851 represents rolling proof of the factory's unshakeable belief in the merits of the 90-degree vee-twin as the ideal configuration for a motorcycle engine. It looks, sounds, rides and feels very different from the ubiquitous Japanese 750cc fours, yet it can match them for power and speed and it can beat them for weight.

The hallmark of a vee-twin is smoothness and torque. The 851 has these qualities in abundance but it also has an extra ingredient – real mid-range strength and power. The computer controlled fuel injection ensures perfect delivery with no flat spots. It'll pull cleanly from 2000rpm with good, low down response. This small and light engine has about the same maximum output as a four-cylinder 750, but the big difference is that the power is spread over a much wider range. The 851's meaty acceleration lives between 6000 and 9000rpm, which is low compared to the dizzy rpm ceilings of Japanese fours. The road bike makes 105hp. A basic, privateer race-kitted version will produce around 112hp while the cossetted and precious works racer pumps 131hp, a truly magnificent figure for a twin. In any guise, the exhaust note is sheer music. At low revs it rumbles and snarls. Once into its high-speed stride, it simply howls. It's a delicious, evocative sound.

The 851's frame is distinctly old-fashioned, being crafted in chrome-moly steel tube rather than in large section aluminium. In its favour, the intricate latticework of tubing is fully triangulated and the critical areas around the steering head and swingarm pivot are strong. The frame uses the engine as a fully stressed member.

Overall, the chassis is compact, small and very light. Top quality Italian Marzocchi suspension is fitted as standard and has particularly well-considered damping rates. The steering benefits from a steep head angle. The brakes have wonderful force and feel – four-piston Brembo calipers biting on fully-floating 320mm discs up front with a single 245mm rear. Maybe its dry weight isn't quite as light as you'd expect for a twin but its various incarnations show how light it can be made. The stock roadster, with all its necessary street-legal running gear, has a dry weight of 181k(398lb). A privately-entered and prepared race-kitted version will scale closer to 360lb (163kg) while the full factory race bike, complete with titanium fasteners pinning together its carbon fibre bodywork, is a lean 330lb (149kg).

Against all the odds, in creating the 851, the small Ducati factory succeeded in building a twin that could beat the world's best four-cylinder bikes. Ducati's philosophy was simple – they needed to be seen competing and winning at the highest level. On numerous tracks the bike has proved faster in a straight line than the Japanese works teams' Honda RC30s and Yamaha OWO1s.

Described accurately by some enthusiasts as the most 'horny' motorcycle in captivity, the 851 roadster is probably the most coveted motorbike of the last ten years (or since the time when some of the great Italian manufacturers like MV Agusta went out of business). Pure, sculptured Italian artistry – power and beauty in plentiful measure.

LAVERDA RGS CORSA

ITALY

ENGINE:
in-line, three-cylinder, DOHC

CUBIC CAPACITY:
981cc

MAXIMUM POWER:
approx. 95bhp at 6500rpm

BORE × STROKE:
75 × 74mm

GEARBOX:
five-speed

FINAL DRIVE:
chain

WHEELBASE:
1524mm (60in)

DRY WEIGHT:
241kg (532lb)

TOP SPEED:
224kph (140mph)

STANDING QUARTER MILE:
12.4sec

DATE OF LAUNCH:
1983

The Laverda lineage is that of a noble late arrival. The brothers Laverda built their first motorcycle, a 750 twin, in the 1960s. With success on the race-tracks, it won them a reputation for high performance and good engineering. Then came the 1000cc triple, typified by the raucous and very rapid Jota. With its 180-degree crankshaft – two pistons up, one down – the first generation triple was also somewhat raw-boned. Some vibration, as well as an enigmatic exhaust note, was the inevitable result.

Laverda eschewed such compromise engineering as balance shafts, and made sure everything was well made and well screwed together. When they tackled the vibration in order to tame the wild thing they had created, they did so with a major re-engineering job.

On the mid-1980s 'second-generation' triples, not only is the engine mounted in rubber, the crankshaft is now 120 degrees (with all pistons evenly spaced). It has smoothed out more than the exhaust note.

The RGS was the result, and the Corsa its sporting incarnation; a bike that clothes the punch of three big pistons in the sleekest of sheaths.

The bike is, as far as possible, a two-wheeled equivalent of a designer Italian sports car, with a twin-camshaft rev-hungry engine and RG-Studios original and aerodynamic bodywork in the classically elegant mode . . . a veritable Ferrari on two wheels. Tell that to a man who is experiencing the high-speed performance of the one-litre Laverda, and he will scoff at the insulated remoteness of a car-borne equivalent. You can really feel 140mph when the wind is plucking at your back, and you can hear the distinctive wail of the robust three-cylinder exhaust note being swallowed up in your wake.

The process of civilization has given the RGS a quieter engine and a more subdued exhaust, to go with the new tailored image, not to mention new noise regulations introduced in the 1980s. Not that the RGS is subdued. With 95 horsepower and a wind-cheating shape, it can run with the best of them, and top 140mph. The Jota's bad manners and vibration (as well as some of its urgency) have gone, replaced by a maturity that has broadened the power band to compensate. The later Laverda engine pulls strongly from low to high revs, and is well-mannered all the way.

Price as well as breeding used to separate the Laverda from the Japanese opposition. It was always significantly more expensive, yet in many ways rather old-fashioned. It had, for example, traditional twin-rear shock absorbers, its Oriental rivals have multi-adjustable rising rate linkages operating single units.

OPPOSITE AND BELOW: Italian style at its most svelte, with bodywork abbreviated to show the robust fins and casings of the air-cooled, three cylinder engine. The original RGS introduced the line. The Corsa, pictured in flight, realised its full 140mph potential.

By 1984 Laverda's performance figures could no longer keep pace with the power war. Worse, their sales figures began to drop alarmingly. The Italian factory at Breganze ran into severe financial difficulties in 1985 and motorcycle production ceased until, with aid from the Italian government, a major reinvestment was finalized in 1989.

Today Laverda are back manufacturing motorcycles, albeit on an even smaller scale than before, with limited resources and development plans. Various new bikes have not got beyond the prototype stage though Laverda aficionados have been heartened by the news of a reworked and more powerful SFC1000 triple. The factory seem to realize their best market is among traditional Laverda connoisseurs. They know that a bike with a good standing-quarter-mile time and a fearsome top speed is not necessarily better at traversing long distances at sustained high average speeds than a well-bred, well-balanced and amply powerful Italian thoroughbred.

MOTO GUZZI LE MANS 1000

The Le Mans has been Moto Guzzi's top sports bike for nearly 15 years. The big bore 1000cc version made a welcome addition to the ranks in 1985, but is essentially similar to the 850 Le Mans they have been producing, virtually unchanged, since 1977. The bike has a fine and enviable reputation as a tried, trusted and proven motorcycle. Its design may be dated and the main features are undeniably conservative and traditional. Reliability above all, however, has won it many friends and admirers.

The 948.8cc OHV Vee-twin engine with its longitudinally-mounted crank and shaft drive is not, by any stretch of the imagination, a high-revving unit. Low down acceleration and pick up is dismal, unaided by unbelievably tall gearing and a dry, twin plate clutch. Once into its mid-range stride though, with the huge 40mm carburettors really roaring, it makes strong and plentiful power. Top end performance is the hallmark of the long-legged Le Mans and the high gearing helps it to a top speed of 140mph with the tachometer barely showing 8000rpm.

Stability and roadholding are very impressive, the bike is surefooted and responsive, a thoroughbred Italian stallion. The double-cradle frame has the sump suspended between the down tubes with the engine weight carried low. Equipped with traditionally harsh, twin shock suspension, the only concession to modern chassis design has been the recent adoption of a 16in front wheel wearing a fatter tyre, making the Le Mans quicker-steering than ever. As befits one of the original café racers, everything about the bike is set purposefully low, making for a keen centre of gravity and a lovely, balanced feel.

Moto Guzzi's integrated braking system is still unique among modern motorcycles and is a boon to safety. The front and rear brakes are linked so that the foot pedal operates both the rear brake and one of the front discs for measured, controlled braking. A special distribution valve directs 70 per cent of the pressure applied to the left hand front disc and the remaining 30 per cent to the rear. The front handlebar lever brakes the right hand front disc but need only be used from very high speeds.

Overall, the Le Mans is a traditional curiously idiosyncratic bike with heavy yet strong controls, an agricultural yet un-burstable engine and redoubtable Italian handling. The paintwork and finish are excellent. It is a sportsman's motorcycle, a high profile and ever popular machine that has long delighted enthusiasts around the world with its tireless performance and peerless reliability.

The essential simplicity of the Guzzi vee-twin engine has encouraged many tuners to tweak more power from the basic four valve unit. As various Battle of the Twins race championships have successfully developed all over Europe and the US, some very hot, individually prepared, back garage racing Guzzis have appeared.

The best of them all perhaps was built and raced by an American dentist, Dr John Wittner, whose cobbled together, big bore, eight valve Guzzi was timed at 162mph coming off the Daytona speedbowl banking in Florida. In honour of what's become known as 'the Dr John Guzzi' the factory have recently begun production of a limited edition replica. Called the Daytona 1000, it's an air-cooled, overhead cam, eight valve 992cc twin, shaft-driven as usual but with un-linked brakes and a single seat. Fully faired, weighing 452lb dry, it's available with either carburettor or fuel injection and is geared to run 152mph off its 94hp. One only hopes it goes into full production – over 150mph from an air-cooled, vee-twin shaft is more than impressive. At full speed, you'd definitely know you were motoring.

BAKKER DUCATI 960

HOLLAND

ENGINE:
Air-cooled, 90-degree,
vee-twin

CUBIC CAPACITY:
960cc

MAXIMUM POWER:
85bhp at 7000rpm

BORE × STROKE:
90 × 74.4mm

GEARBOX:
five-speed

FINAL DRIVE:
roller chain

WHEELBASE:
1472mm (58in)

DRY WEIGHT:
210kg (463lb)

TOP SPEED:
224kph (140mph)

STANDING QUARTER MILE:
12.6sec

DATE OF LAUNCH:
1988

The assembly of this magnificent motorcycle was planned, projected, co-ordinated and executed to a remarkable degree. The work took over a year and involved 23 companies in five countries resulting in a five figure bill. It is one of the cleanest motor-cycles ever seen. There isn't a visible part that hasn't been highly-polished and beneath every bright bolt and shiny screw there lurks a polished washer. It bristles with bright-work, shimmering with excellence and attention to detail. It is a stunning, immaculate-looking motorcycle.

It belongs to Gerhard Klein, an enthusiast who had an idea to combine the timeless, thunder road appeal of a large Ducati desmo vee-twin with the most modern rolling chassis available. He spent a lot of time visualizing the con-cept and pouring over component catalogues. It was his vision and he controlled the project, though various experts did the work.

Most of the assembly was done by Newton Equipment, a London based shop specializing in building bespoke Ducatis. The heart of the bike is a 946cc engine, an ex-900SS lump which Newton's mechanics knew to be a good one. It had been kept in the family and had a known history.

This engine has been extensively revised. The vee-twin beat is now pumped by 90mm Mahle racing pistons riding in Nicasil-coated Borchardt aluminium liners. Down below, there's a special crank, much lightened and balanced. Up top, large valves ride on stock cams and desmo gear but the heads, ports and valve-train have all been polished and honed to perfection. The carbs are standard 40mm Dellortos. The front exhaust pipes had to be homemade and custom-bent to suit the frame and match the Nico Bakker mufflers. The starter motor was consigned to the dustbin because Gerhard was adamant that his Ducati must be kicked into life.

The inside of the crankcase was machined out to take a new hydraulic, lightweight clutch. All external engine sur-faces, including the crankcases, were highly-polished. The cylinder heads were beadblasted and any hint of tackiness, like plastic breathers, the manifold spacers and the original bevel tubes, was swiftly replaced by aluminium parts. The gearbox is stock but the engine changes are reckoned to be worth 85hp at the rear tyre.

Gerhard travelled a lot of miles looking for a chassis including visits to Harris Performance in Hertfordshire, Borchardt in Aachen and Egli in Switzerland. He finally found what he wanted at Nico Bakker's in Holland — a 40×80mm aluminium deltabox frame that was simple, strong, rigid and light. Unfortunately, Nico only made them for Japanese and BMW engines. But when Gerhard showed

OPPOSITE: One of the cleanest bikes ever built, Gerhard Klein's Bakker Ducati successfully combines a classic Ducati engine with a modern, sophisticated rolling chassis. ***INSET, ABOVE AND BELOW:*** The rider's eye view — note the magnesium fork yokes and white-faced Veglia clocks — plus how the immaculately-restored 946 vee-twin lump is hung from the Bakker beam frame. The brakes are fully-floating, four-piston Brembos. The fairing is from a much-modified Paso.

him photos of his newly-completed Ducati engine, Nico agreed to develop a new frame just to house this one special motor.

On completing the basic chassis, Nico kitted it out with 42mm Marzocchi ML 1 forks held by Bakker magnesium-aluminium racing yokes with a rising-rate, rear linkage feeding an 11-way adjustable White Power shock. The electrics are all rubber-mounted on a single plate carried underneath the hand-built aluminium petrol tank. The wheels are 17 and 18in, hollow-cast, three-spoke, aluminium made by Braun and Boegel in Germany and fitted with fat Michelin radial tyres. The brakes are fully-floating, four-piston Brembos.

Harris Performance made the seat which is covered in expensive Connolly leather specially dyed. Instrumentation is confined to white-faced Veglia 'competizione' tacho and speedo clocks on an aluminium carrier with Tomaselli 2000

adjustable bars plus standard Ducati switchgear. The fairing is a much-modified top half of one from a Ducati Paso. The paint is fluorescent, acrylic and totally exclusive. A special pigmentation was supplied by Swada in Wales. The bike is so colourful, striking and plain tricky, it's not at all easy to light and photograph. It's not yellow, it's green but its wonderful hues change all the time.

Every part of it has been polished and buffed into brilliance. All the suspension components, the yokes, the sprockets, every single part has had an appointment with a battery of air-polishers including such minute details as the tiny anti-dive reservoir on the front fork and the *inside* of the drilled holes in the brake discs. Needless to say the bike has won many concours awards and its fortunate owner is one happy and proud man. He says it rides and sounds like a dream, and he only dares to take it out on perfectly dry and sunny days.

HONDA VFR750R (RC30)

The VFR750R (or RC30) is the most exotic street bike Honda have ever built. It is a direct descendant of Honda's all-conquering RVF750 factory endurance racer which has proved virtually unbeatable in long distance racing since 1985.

With the advent of World Superbike racing in 1988, Honda along with the other manufacturers, had to build expensive, limited edition street bikes in order to comply with the production-based rules. The RC30 was their World Superbike offering. It won the championship for rider Fred Merkel in 1988 and 1989 and has since proved the most popular mount in all forms of 750cc competition, be it Formula-One, Superbike or endurance racing.

Hand-built at the rate of 60 a week, the RC30 is an exquisitely detailed machine that encompasses everything Honda have ever learnt from 15 years and thousands of miles of endurance racing. Its heart is a vee-four engine with a 360-degree crankshaft and some distinctive power characteristics. The power output offers exceptional torque and traction. The delivery is smooth and plentiful (the torque curve is flat from 7500rpm to 11,500rpm) aiding tyre feel. Gear driven cams precisely control valve operation and contribute to the wonderful, growling noise it makes when fully wound up. The gearbox is a close-ratio, six-speeder which means a very high first gear. The clutch needs to be slipped to get moving and while it'll never win any drag races, hitting the redline in first gear means a speed of 75mph or nearly half its maximum speed in top gear.

The rolling chassis perfectly matches the engine and gives the bike impressive balance plus outstanding roadholding and ride feel. The riding position as well as the handling are often near perfect. Compactly designed with a short wheelbase, a keen weight and superb suspension, the RC30 really is a scratchers delight. The twin spar aluminium frame uses the engine as a stressed member and sports a single-sided swingarm of massive section (it was originally developed on the Honda-Elf works endurance racer of the early 1980s). The suspension front and rear is by multi-adjustable Showa units. The brakes are by Nissin with four-piston calipers. Endurance racing touches abound – like quickly-detachable wheels and front brakes. Expensive engineering is everywhere – the hand-laid fibreglass, the titanium con-rods, the magnesium engine covers, the roller bearing cams, the aluminium gas tank and the sand-cast aluminium swingarm and steering head.

Available only in HRC (Honda Racing Corporation) colours of red, white and blue and strictly solo, the RC30 is as complete a racer-for-the-road as we're ever likely to see. It's built with racetrack precision in mind and it's been

OPPOSITE ABOVE: Pictured here in HRC (Honda Racing Corporation) colours of red, white and blue, the RC30 has proved the mainstay of four-stroke racing competition world-wide. The compact and finely-detailed chassis perfectly matches the powerful vee-four engine.

OPPOSITE BELOW: The RC30 in action shows the advantage of having a single-sided swingarm and a quickly-detachable rear wheel.

assembled as precisely as an expensive Swiss watch.

Honda make a similar vee-four roadster for the masses called the VFR750F. It, too, sports gear driven cams and a torquey motor which is housed in a twin-spar aluminium frame with a single-sided swingarm. The specifications are similar but the performance and the ride are wholly different. The RC30 represents everything Honda have learnt in 20 years of four-stroke racing. Many experts consider it the finest bike ever built and certainly the best they're ever likely to ride.

HONDA CBR1000F

JAPAN

ENGINE:
Liquid-cooled, DOHC in-line
four

CUBIC CAPACITY:
998cc

MAXIMUM POWER:
132bhp at 9500rpm

BORE × STROKE:
77 × 53.6mm

GEARBOX:
six-speed

FINAL DRIVE:
roller chain

WHEELBASE:
150mm (59.1in)

DRY WEIGHT:
222kg (490lb)

TOP SPEED:
257kph (161mph)

STANDING QUARTER MILE:
11.1sec

DATE OF LAUNCH:
1987

The CBR1000 is Honda's flagship sports roadster. It is not a race replica. It excels at being a versatile, all-rounder, sports-angled for sure, but also sensibly equipped with just about everything the fast long-distance rider requires. Call it a deluxe highway express cruiser.

Released in 1987 to universal acclaim, the CBR1000 broke no new ground but underlined the world's largest manufacturer's 20 years of experience at building in-line fours. It is very much a complete motorcycle. The design brief was to build a 1000cc open class sports bike for the road rider. It had to be powerful, comfortable, smooth and sophisticated with styling to match. Honda succeeded on all counts.

The soul of the machine is a fairly conventional short stroke, 16-valve in-line four fed by semi-downdraft Keihin CV carbs. About the only thing that distinguishes it from the many such in-line fours Honda have produced before is the remote oil-cooled generator mounted behind the cylinders. As with the whole bike, what impresses about the engine is not what it is but what it does. For a start, it's uncannily smooth. There's no discernible vibration except at the very top of its rev range. It also combines what every engine tuner likes – fat, endless torque with a real top end rev rush.

The big Honda is very tractable. It'll pull top gear from 2000rpm and you can short-shift and stay in top for most day-to-day unhurried riding. It starts making huge liquid power at 6000rpm with a step at 8000 where the engine spins like crazy up to the 10,500rpm redline. You can cruise leisurely on the torque or you can burn rubber by spinning it out above 8000. Sensibly geared with six fairly close ratios, its top speed is 160mph.

The race replicas will certainly beat it for top end and they'll outhandle it on a tight road. However the Honda will never be that far behind and it possesses in abundance what all the sparse, narrow-focus, race replicas lack, which is a high degree of ride comfort.

Again, there is nothing particularly innovative about the rolling chassis, it just all works together and well. The perimeter frame is old-fashioned steel and there's nothing radical about the steering geometry. Suspension is generally soft and only really firms up over the last few inches of travel. The ride is plush and best suited to wide-open sweeping roads. Similarly, the steering is slow but it's also predictable. The Honda can be slammed through a series of quick bends as long as you're deliberate about where you place the front wheel. Slow steering and heavy it may be, but that front end is also very trustworthy. It stays planted on the road. Wheel rim sizes are as big as they come at 3.5in front and 5.5in rear and the elegant, three-spoke

OPPOSITE ABOVE AND BELOW:
The culmination of 20 years experience at building in-line fours, the CBR1000 sports-tourer is distinguished by effortless, almost majestic performance. A road rider's machine par excellence.

wheels wear fat radial tyres.

Thanks to an excellent riding position, ride comfort is assured. There's plenty of room for a pillion and luggage. The aerodynamically efficient ABS fairing fits like a glove and there are no gaps or ill-fitting joins in its smooth lines – even the exhaust pipes get their own fairing cover. The bodywork is protected by unobtrusive 'bamper dampers' which is curious Japanese-speak for metal bumpers with soft plastic covers. If the bike falls over at low speed, the bumper protects the expensive bodywork.

Detail touches abound and the bike is superbly well-finished. The key to the CBR1000's success is that it's much more than the sum of its parts. In isolation, its major components are well-made but unexceptional. But as a rolling package the motorcycle exudes confidence, balance and completeness. A motorcycle for all reasons and all seasons and the best in-line four Honda have ever made.

JAPAN

ENGINE:
Liquid-cooled, DOHC
vee-four

CUBIC CAPACITY:
1084cc

MAXIMUM POWER:
100bhp at 7500rpm

BORE × STROKE:
73 × 64.8mm

GEARBOX:
five-speed

FINAL DRIVE:
shaft

WHEELBASE:
1550mm (61.1in)

DRY WEIGHT:
279kg (615lb)

TOP SPEED:
230kph (144mph)

STANDING QUARTER MILE:
11.3sec

DATE OF LAUNCH:
1990

Although this bike was built in Japan, it was designed and styled in Europe with input from Honda agencies in Britain, France and, particularly, Germany. The Europeans specified that they wanted a bike that could cover long distances carrying heavy loads at high speed in supreme comfort, yet wasn't so firmly cast in the touring mode that it couldn't offer some sports thrills and everyday enjoyment as well. They were after a big, easy handling, distinctly styled and equipped all-rounder especially built for Europe. The ST1100 Pan-European is what Honda in Japan delivered – a long distance deluxe Eurocruiser.

The key to the ST1100 is not high speed as such but sustained high speed. The design brief demanded that the rider must be able to spend three hours in the saddle without discomfort. So the ST comes with a large, spacious saddle, a big full fairing and windscreen, an ample 28litre fuel tank plus 35litre panniers and a comfy, studied riding position. It also comes with a large 1084cc vee-four engine specially built for long distance operation.

The engine is quiet, smooth, vibration-free and flexible. Longitudinally mounted, the 360-degree crankshaft benefits from a direct driveline to the final driveshaft. The crank runs a balancer to help even out the big 360-degree pulses. The driveline contains numerous dampers. The dual camshafts are belt-driven. All these details reduce vibration and noise and enhance smooth operation.

The engine is not restricted to 100hp but is in a fairly low state of tune. Redline is set at a conservative 8000rpm, although the unit will rev up to its limiter at 9500. Peak torque is a mighty 75ft/lb at 6500rpm. It is very understressed and the power it produces is fatly spread and perfectly suited to the long distance work intended. The vee-four engine is noted for its torque and traction. The ST harnesses really usable power, meaning you can cruise all day at 130mph in comfort rather than in a blur of revs. It's been designed to haul a big touring load at speed without overloading the engine.

The steel frame does a fairly conventional job in housing the big engine – the bottom frame rails ride above the crankcases to help keep the engine weight and the centre of gravity low in the chassis. Similarly the huge 6.2 gallon fuel tank carries the gas low down under the seat (what looks like the petrol tank is a dummy cover). But its overall dry weight is still high at 623lb and pushing it around with a dead engine or heaving it on to its centrestand provides an instant reminder of its considerable poundage.

Once on the move though, the ST offers both a stately and sprightly ride. The action of the 41mm front forks and

OPPOSITE ABOVE AND BELOW:
Honda's first big bike to be designed in Europe, the ST1100 Pan-European comes well-equipped for the long-distance road.

INSET: The comfortable riding position and cockpit instrumentation including the useful headlight beam adjuster.

single shock rear suspension are well-suited to the long distance road, allowing lots of wheel travel and giving a plush ride. Touring details abound – the 28 litre fuel tank is good for over 250 miles before refuelling, the panniers are large enough to carry a full face helmet, the screen has adjustable vents to avoid high speed turbulence in varying conditions. There are well thought out detail touches too – like front fork covers to prevent stone chipping and pannier mount covers that fold down when the panniers are removed. The panniers themselves have toughened bases to prevent scratching when on the ground. The ST inherits the 'bamper-damper' crash bars first seen on the CBR1000 that ensure you don't have to replace the whole fairing if the bike falls over. The integrated mirror/indicator assemblies are designed to 'pop off' in the event of impact, avoiding fairing damage. They then just 'pop' back on again. The fairing has stash pouches for maps and the tool kit. The excellent instrumentation has a useful headlight beam adjustment knob. Finally, there are sympathetic mechanical considerations – the plugs and oil filter are easy to remove, access to the clutch is particularly straightforward.

Targeted against various BMWs and Yamaha's evergreen FJ1200, the ST1100 Pan-European is every inch a sports-touring flagship, a first-rate machine with a thoroughly re-searched design brief based on what European riders wanted from a big bike. It comes equipped with an excel-lently detailed specification. Just the sort of bike that en-courages you to go home the long way. Around the world.

JAPAN

ENGINE:
Liquid-cooled, SOHC Flat-six

CUBIC CAPACITY:
1520cc

MAXIMUM POWER:
100bhp at 5200rpm

BORE × STROKE:
71 × 64mm

GEARBOX:
five-speed

FINAL DRIVE:
shaft

WHEELBASE:
1700mm (66.9in)

DRY WEIGHT:
365kg (804lb)

TOP SPEED:
193kph (121mph)

STANDING QUARTER MILE:
13.2sec

DATE OF LAUNCH:
1988

On the move, it is not the size of the GL1500 that is the most obvious thing. It is the smooth and fluid engine; its capability of running at well over the ton for mile after mile, never straining, always comfortable, and never, ever, feeling short of power.

Honda's Gold Wing of the mid-1970s started big and kept getting bigger. In its original form it was an unfaired machine, and the liquid-cooled flat four engine displaced 1000cc. At that time, nobody had seen anything quite so enormous.

It was not long before luxury touring riders in the USA started fitting out their Gold Wings for the long haul down Easy Street. Their requirements gave birth to an accessory industry supplying everything from super-soft 'King and Queen' seats to gigantic fairings with matching three-piece luggage equipment, as well as air suspension to smooth the ride to the standards of a family car.

The 1983 1200cc Aspencade (named after the biggest gathering of touring riders in the USA) was Honda's answer. It came equipped with *everything*. With panniers and a gigantic top box, you could load luggage enough for three. Want to take the barbecue? Load it right on.

A massive fairing offered not only complete weather protection but was built to the highest standards, with plenty of lock-up storage compartments and a ventilation system. A full stereo radio and tape player added music to the passing zephyr. The engine certainly made no noise loud enough to drown it.

Honda also installed their own air suspension – with an extra refinement. An on-board compressor was built into the bike and the suspension could be made harder or softer without even stopping: firming the ride up for more stability when swinging through the mountain bends, and then softening it to a lulling wallow on the long straights through the deserts.

All this was carried through to the latest model – the 1988 GL1500, the ultimate full dresser and with a major engine change. Bigger than ever, the new Gold Wing's motive power is now a flat, six-cylinder engine.

The gross tonnage of the Gold Wing is rarely a problem on the roll. Despite limited ground clearance this behemoth is quite nimble and handy on a tight road as long as the rider doesn't get too enthusiastic and let the huge rolling mass run away from his control. The silky-smooth, turbine-like engine redlines at a low 5500rpm, makes enormous torque (110ft/lbs) and retains healthy acceleration from low to high speeds as well as an ability to cruise relatively economically in its overdrive top gear. With shaft drive and that big, lazy engine, maintenance is an infrequent chore.

OPPOSITE ABOVE AND BELOW: The only six-cylinder motorcycle in production, Honda's GL1500 Gold Wing is the ultimate in luxury tourers. Surprisingly nimble on the move, it comes equipped with a handy reverse gear to help manoeuvre 365kg of motorcycle at parking speeds.

The Gold Wing was developed with long distances as well as high speeds in mind. It will keep on running as long as its pampered and cosseted rider wants it to.

There is a huge array of gadgetry to play with. The current model sports a 25-watt, full logic audio system with presets, auto scanning, auto volume levelling and CB radio function. Then there's cruise control, climate control, a two-way intercom, adjustable pegs (with foot warming options) plus both analogue and digital display information for speed, rpm, temperature, fuel level, time, audio functions and suspension pressures.

The latest innovation on the 1500, and one fully acknowledging its dead weight, is a reverse gear, operated off the starter motor at low speeds and designed purely to help park the motorcycle since pushing or rolling it backwards is no longer a task for mere mortals.

The Gold Wing always was designed primarily for the USA and is as American as a Japanese bike can be. Honda by-pass import restrictions by assembling Gold Wings in their own US factory. Also popular in Europe, the Gold Wing has spawned numerous imitations from Japanese rivals but remains in a class of its own. Honda did it first and the bike is still the definitive heavyweight luxury tourer. For over 15 years now Honda have kept faithful to the Gold Wing tradition of giving you an awful lot of motorcycle for your money.

KAWASAKI ZZ-R600

JAPAN

ENGINE:
Liquid-cooled, DOHC in-line four

CUBIC CAPACITY:
599cc

MAXIMUM POWER:
98bhp at 11,500rpm

BORE × STROKE:
64 × 46.6mm

GEARBOX:
six-speed

FINAL DRIVE:
roller chain

WHEELBASE:
1440mm (56.7in)

DRY WEIGHT:
195kg (429lb)

TOP SPEED:
233kph (146mph)

STANDING QUARTER MILE:
11.7sec

DATE OF LAUNCH:
1990

There has been a refreshing move towards middleweight motorcycles in the last few years – lighter, smaller 600cc bikes that, thanks to development and competition between the major manufacturers, are now every bit as fast and exciting as the 750cc motorcycles of the late 1980s. The current 600cc class leader is Kawasaki's ZZ-R600, a 98hp rev-happy four with an incredible 14,000rpm redline and a compact, competent chassis.

Kawasaki are normally deadly serious about being top of every capacity class they compete in, yet they chose not to make the ZZ-R an out-and-out 600cc sports bike. 'Make it classy *and* comfortable' was the design brief. It had to be 'generously proportioned, offering day-long comfort *and* performance'. Physically quite large with plenty of room for the tall rider, the ZZ-R sits on radially tyred 17in wheels, has comfortable to use, neutrally steering handlebars and an all-up dry weight of 429lb. It's the first Kawasaki 600 to run an aluminium main frame, the perimeter layout of which is unusual in that it features two bracing side-rails (or downtubes) which run off the two main box-section beams, acting as two of the six engine mounts.

At the rear, the large-section aluminium swingarm uses ZXR-750-spec bearings at the pivot. The 41mm front forks are from the ZX-10. The bodywork and seat echo its bigger brother, the mighty ZZ-R1100 in being sleek, functional and large. It handles superbly – light, sharp, flickable and fairly effortless – it's one of those bikes you really can ride the wheels off.

Despite its dizzy 14,000rpm redline, the motor's power is not confined just to the top end. The engine makes strong, smooth power throughout the mid-range and the 14,000rpm rev ceiling is largely there for racing development and application. The road bike will rev that high safely but the power is tailing off by 12,500rpm.

The engine specification is impressive. Oversquare, short stroking and running high 11.5:1 compression, they've taken advantage of the compact cylinder head (10mm spark plugs, tight combustion chambers and narrow included valve angles) by using different bore tappets (the exhaust ones are smaller). Valve sizes are large and the valve seats are hand-finished. The 36mm Keihin carbs feature semi-flat slides and get a straight shot at the intake ports of the slightly inclined engine. The carbs are fed by an airbox bigger than that fitted to the ZX-10. Digital ignition times the sparks precisely.

At the bottom end, the crankshaft runs on six plain bearings ensuring strong, vibration-free power delivery. Engine heat is kept under control by dual oil pumps and cleverly routed coolant passages in the cylinder head. The rider gets to know all about the engine's dynamic performance by a short action throttle. The power is free-flowing, plentiful and fast, and with the rider fully tucked-in behind the generous fairing the ZZ-R will stretch to a top speed just shy of 150mph.

In six years of 600cc production, Kawasaki have raised outright power output from 75hp (on their original pioneering GPZ600) to nearly 100hp on the ZZ-R. A straight 25 per cent improvement, enough to give the ZZ-R the best all-round performance ever seen in the 600cc roadster class. Its big brother, the ZZ-R1100 is currently king of the litre-plus class and fully deserves its sobriquet, ZZ Top. But the 600 is proof positive that good things really do come in small packages.

JAPAN

ENGINE:
Liquid-cooled, DOHC in-line four

CUBIC CAPACITY:
748cc

MAXIMUM POWER:
108bhp at 10,500rpm

BORE × STROKE:
68 × 51.5mm

GEARBOX:
six-speed

FINAL DRIVE:
roller chain

WHEELBASE:
1455mm (57.3in)

DRY WEIGHT:
200kg (441lb)

TOP SPEED:
243kph (152mph)

STANDING QUARTER MILE:
11.1sec

DATE OF LAUNCH:
1989

The ZXR750 is Kawasaki's entry-level World Superbike contender for the racer on a budget. It is also a very fine sports roadster. Instead of building expensive limited edition World Superbike specials like Honda's RC30 and Yamaha's OWO1, Kawasaki decided to mass manufacture a cheaper, more basic 750 that they could sell to the ordinary motorcyclist. Race kits are available for the track fiends but essentially the ZXR is a road bike that can be transformed into a racer, not the other way round.

Limited edition specials have never interested Kawasaki and their decision to mass produce the ZXR at reasonable cost led to a refreshing design brief. Instead of assembling an expensive, hugely powerful engine, they only mildly tuned their GPX750 road bike engine. They then installed it in a trick, all new sports chassis with styling that made it look like the factory endurance racer. That way racers who wanted tuned engines could spend money on the factory racekits while the road rider got a proven motor in a new, sharp handling package.

That the ZXR750 only produced 108hp compared to the 106hp of the much older and traditionally styled GPX750 proved a disappointment to some people. It shouldn't have done because the ZXR's cycle parts allow all of the 108hp to be enjoyed to the hilt. The ZXR is one of the few modern 750s that can be ridden to its maximum in comparative safety. Even without blinding horsepower it provides maximum riding thrills.

The suspension, although multi-adjustable, is sports stiff and this, combined with the cramped and spartan riding position, can be punishing on anything but dead smooth roads. The rider is stretched over the high and wide tank to the clip-on handlebars. The seat is hard and any bumps initially absorbed by the harsh springing tend to be transmitted through to the rider's chest and crotch.

That aside, once the suspension and ride height have been set up to suit the individual and the terrain, the ZXR is very surefooted, stable and predictable. The steering is definitely not quick but its neutral to heavy action encourages hanging-off with the rider transferring his weight around the turns like a real racer. The slightly top heavy feel disappears at speed. Above 100mph the enforced riding position starts working for the rider, the wind lifting the pressure off the wrists and the handling becoming increasingly lively and responsive.

The engine was extensively revised in 1990 and features a lot of parts previously only available in the racekit. Fed by big, semi-downdraft carbs, the current model wears a new cylinder head, larger valves and smaller, lighter pistons. The factory's engine tuners have extended both the powerband

OPPOSITE CENTRE AND BELOW: **Kawasaki's ZXR750 is a race replica for the road that can be kitted for the track.**

OPPOSITE, FAR RIGHT: **Styled like a factory endurance racer with twin headlights, the twin air intakes route cooling air to the cylinder head via the distinctive twin hoses that pass through the tank.**

and top end horsepower, though it remains an engine that has to be revved hard to give of its best.

Equipped with typically strong Kawasaki brakes and excellently finished with quality paint and snug-fitting bodywork, the ZXR is an interesting variation of the race-replica theme offering a proven roadster engine in a race-orientated chassis. Strangely, the kitted versions run by privateers in World Superbike races have struggled against the much more expensive RC30s, OWO1s and Ducati 851s. The factory have a moderately successful Formula-One spec version called the ZX7 Stinger but that's a hand-built, mega-expensive raceshop creation bearing little resemblance to the mass produced bike.

JAPAN

ENGINE:
Liquid-cooled, DOHC in-line
four

CUBIC CAPACITY:
997cc

MAXIMUM POWER:
135bhp at 10,500rpm

BORE × STROKE:
74 × 58mm

GEARBOX:
six-speed

FINAL DRIVE:
roller chain

WHEELBASE:
1490mm (58.7in)

DRY WEIGHT:
222kg (489lb)

TOP SPEED:
265kph (166mph)

STANDING QUARTER MILE:
11.3sec

DATE OF LAUNCH:
1988

Two years is a long time in motorcycling. It seems ridiculous to think that this motorcycle is now considered slightly old-fashioned but it has certainly been superseded. It retains its place in this book for several important reasons. Until Kawasaki launched a yet more powerful motorcycle in 1990, the ZX-10 was the undisputed heavyweight champ. The fastest production motorcycle in the world bar none. Kawasaki have always known that to have the accredited fastest bike is to have a guaranteed best-seller and from 1988-90, the ZX-10 enjoyed a remarkable reign at the head of litre-plus bike sales. That, in 1990, the factory chose to release a faster version of the ZX-10, called the ZZ-R1100, surprised nobody. The ZX-10 itself replaced the RX1000 of 1986 and *that* was the fastest production roadster of its time. In 1986, Kawasaki had publicly declared that they would never build a more powerful motorbike. By 1990 they had reneged on their power promises twice and few were complaining. Kawasaki Heavy Industries have been dedicated to perfecting the in-line four cylinder motorcycle engine for 18 years now and it was inevitable that they would find new ways of extracting more power for less weight.

That it has been replaced by a top line motorcycle from the same manufacturer is perhaps ignominious for the ZX-10. Yet it remains available, popular and deserving of inclusion because it is a big, uncompromising bruiser of a motorcycle capable of performance figures that still stand up in the big numbers world of real superbikes.

A stock ZX-10 will hit 160mph, no problem. Derestricted and rejetted with gearing to match, it'll touch 170mph, which is not exactly an old-fashioned speed. The maximum power output is restricted in various markets by carb tops that prevent full throttle slide lift and full bore motorcycling. The engine was designed as a full 135bhp unit, developed from the older RX1000, but with a lot of work concentrating on increasing intake and combustion efficiency while lightening engine components throughout.

The power it produces is smooth and huge. There is no real step to the power until 8000rpm and since 7500rpm in top gear gives a road speed of 115mph, it's easy to take the power for granted since there's always so much of it available. The output really jumps from 8000 to 11,000rpm, yet the motor is safe, dependable and always smooth, even when caned. Fuel efficient and devastatingly quick, the ZX-10 motor has but one unfortunate glitch – an annoying flat spot between 3500 and 4000rpm where it is unable to take more than quarter throttle. It's irritating because 4000rpm is *50-60mph* in top, just the sort of speed you'd normally hold.

Maybe it's best to head for the open road. The ZX-10

makes for a versatile performer and is surprisingly comfortable, increasingly so at speed, and if the rider always bears in mind its size and inevitable weight, it is very sporting. The E-box frame features a cast steering head and swing-arm pivot welded to extruded box-section beams. The 'E' stands for egg-box, a humble object renowned for its structural rigidity. The egg in this case refers to the shape of the main beams that embrace the engine. The construction is ideal for handling the immense lateral loads the powerful motor feeds into the frame, trying to twist it. It is incredibly wide, yet making it narrower but still strong would increase the wheelbase still further, resulting in a less manoeuvrable bike.

As it is, the ZX-10 handles just fine, it's a touch soft-bellied and you need to be fairly brutal, always gassing it hard to get the best out of its handling. The ride has a vague, detached feel with little feedback from the tyres. Perhaps this is for the best, since the 530lb wet weight of the ZX-10 is disguised somewhat by the generally plush suspension. In its favour, it comes equipped with enormously powerful yet rider-sensitive brakes.

In 1990 it is easy to overlook the ZX-10 as yet another also-ran. In fact it is still a very competitive motorcycle. That big fairing is efficient at deflecting the wind and weather at 120mph, the comfortable riding position makes it a good long-distance mount and its bulk means you can carry quite a lot of luggage. No longer the heavyweight champion, it is merely a living legend. So it goes. Development goes on at the speed of life and all too suddenly, 166mph is last year's performance ceiling and last years motorcycle. But there is nothing old-fashioned about the ZX-10's 135bhp or its popular image as a monster of wheelspin and pure, unadulterated brute force.

JAPAN

ENGINE:
Liquid-cooled, DOHC in-line four

CUBIC CAPACITY:
1052cc

MAXIMUM POWER:
145bhp at 10,500rpm

BORE × STROKE:
76 × 58mm

GEARBOX:
six-speed

FINAL DRIVE:
roller chain

WHEELBASE:
1480mm (58.2in)

DRY WEIGHT:
228kg (503lb)

TOP SPEED:
280kph (175mph)

STANDING QUARTER MILE:
10.2sec

DATE OF LAUNCH:
1990

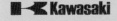

Back in 1985 Kawasaki launched the GPZ1000R (also known as the 1000RX) and said they would never build a quicker bike. Making 125hp and a top speed of 162mph, Kawasaki claimed the 1000RX would 'outperform competing 1000cc-plus super-bikes for some years'. By 1988 Kawasaki had been forced to think again. The other Japanese manufacturers now had 160mph litre-plus bikes and Kawasaki Heavy Industries had to release a new machine to protect their traditional territory as the kings of top speed and fast engines.

That bike was the ZX-10. It, too, ran 162mph but was lighter and generally sportier than the 1000RX it replaced. By 1990, the other manufacturers were still extracting more speed and refinement from their big bikes; Kawasaki obviously decided the ZX-10's impressive credentials were no longer quite good enough because they unveiled yet another world's fastest candidate – the 175mph ZZ-R1100.

A top speed in excess of 170mph represents a quantum leap in outright motorcycle performance. Currently the ZZ-R1100 is one of two candidates for the title of the fastest road bike on the planet. The other is the very expensive and exclusive Bimota Tuatara. Certainly, the ZZ-R is the fastest motorcycle in mass production, a fact that makes its design and engineering almost as impressive as its awesome performance.

A top speed of 175mph requires an awful lot of horse-power. For certain markets, like the UK, the ZZ-R is restricted to a voluntary manufacturer's horsepower limit of 125 (the restriction is a simple device that restricts full carb slide lift and it can be easily removed). For other markets, like the USA and Italy, the motor is sold as it was developed, as a full house, fearsomely powerful engine producing 145bhp.

The engine is a large bore ZX-10 based unit with big valves, large carbs, hand-finished ports, huge cooling requirements and a high 11,500rpm red-line. What really distinguishes it from numerous large capacity, in-line four cylinder motors is a ram-air intake system based on technology borrowed from Formula-One cars. At the front of the bike just below the headlight is an intake that runs back to the 15 litre airbox by a sealed duct. This has two notable effects. First, sealed and isolated from the considerable engine heat, the huge 40mm Keihin carbs are always supplied with nice cool, dense air for good cylinder filling and clean, efficient combustion. Second, the faster the motorcycle goes, the more air it rams in, creating high pressure in the airbox – the result is more airflow, more power, more speed. Put simply, it makes more power the faster you go. And that power is smooth, instant and almost limitless. Above 6000rpm it doesn't so much accelerate as explode.

The only mass-produced motorcycle to wear a 200mph speedo wasn't designed as a race-replica. Kawasaki label it a Sports-Tourer and the chassis complements its dual-purpose ambitions. Rider and pillion are well catered for with a sensible riding position, plenty of room, a low and plush saddle, flat bars, a grab rail and a centrestand.

Although the ZZ-R is inevitably heavier than the ZX-10, the weight has been kept low and the bike is surprisingly manageable and easy to ride.

Big numbers abound — 43mm forks, 310mm front discs and a 170-60 × 17in rear tyre. The aluminium perimeter frame and swingarm have been beefed up considerably from the ZX-10 in order to harness the phenomenal power. Aerodynamically, the bike is a vast improvement with a smoothly contoured fairing and a curiously bulbous tail section.

That the bike is so well mannered and rideable is a tribute to Kawasaki's designers. That it has acceleration and a top speed way in excess of anything else on offer from the major manufacturers merely serves to underline their reputation as the builders of the world's most powerful motorcycle engines. This bike sets a performance standard that will be hard to match let alone beat.

SUZUKI GSX-R750

JAPAN

ENGINE:
Air and oil-cooled, DOHC
in-line four

CUBIC CAPACITY:
749cc

MAXIMUM POWER:
114bhp at 11,000rpm

BORE × STROKE:
70 × 48.7mm

GEARBOX:
six-speed

FINAL DRIVE:
roller chain

WHEELBASE:
1415mm (55.7in)

DRY WEIGHT:
193kg (425lb)

TOP SPEED:
248kph (155mph)

STANDING QUARTER MILE:
10.7sec

DATE OF LAUNCH:
1985

This is the bike that started the street legal racer revolution. Back in 1985 it simply had no competition – it was unique, a race bike in the thinnest possible disguise. An out-of-the-crate, works replica racer that was released to the public and the serious professional at the same time. In its first year on the market, the GSX-R won several important races and championships and nobody from road rider to World Endurance or Formula-One pilot complained about its level of performance or competitiveness. Suzuki called it a Hyper-Sports machine meaning that it was above, over or in excess of what would normally be expected from a 750cc motorcycle. Back in 1985, the GSX-R made 100hp and weighed but 388lb. It was the bike of the year, no question.

Since then there have been numerous changes and at least six different models. Once it stood alone without competition, now it is swamped by other manufacturer's 750cc race replicas. To keep pace, Suzuki have had to find more power. Increasing horsepower needs a stronger, regrettably heavier, rolling chassis to house such a potent motor. The current 1990, GSX-R750L now makes 114hp and weighs 425lb.

Over the years, the changing specification has favoured the road rider more than the racer. The motor had gone from the original long-stroke to a short-stroke version that wouldn't tolerate upping the compression ratio. Now it's back to the original bore × stroke dimensions. The GSX-R750 is certainly the most developed of any current motorcycle engine. Few others have benefited from the almost constant attention, fettling and tuning, redesigning and refining, that Suzuki's pioneering oil-cooled lump has enjoyed. Today a reliable and proven powerhouse of a motor is the result. It has never been endowed with a lot of torque but is characterized by a truly fierce top end making huge power between 8500 and 11,000rpm.

Visually distinguished by its fine pitch cylinder finning, the engine is oil-cooled using pumps and injectors to circulate and spray high volumes of oil through special tubes, passageways and galleries to the hot spots of the engine. For example, to the tops of the combustion chambers and the underside of the piston crowns. A large oil cooler (from the GSX-R1100) takes care of the extra cooling needs, it's beautifully fabricated and curved in shape just to allow Suzuki's chassis engineers to achieve the wheelbase and weight distribution they wanted. Because the engine is air and oil-cooled rather than water-cooled, the GSX-R is characteristically noisy and a bit rough low down and in the mid-range. Yet at the top end the vibration mirrors out. At speed, it's smooth and dead stable. Tucked in behind the

OPPOSITE: Suzuki's GSX-R750 was the original racer with lights. Over five years and six models Suzuki have revised and refined the bike to a remarkable degree. A perennial favourite it is still top of its class – a true sportsman's motorbike.

screen, the forward-biased riding position, dictated by its high and rear set footpegs, really starts working for the rider, as the bike stretches effortlessly to its top speed of 155mph.

As with the engine, a lot of attention has been paid to the frame and suspension over the years. The GSX-R's frame differs from other 750s in not using very large section aluminium beams between the steering head and swingarm pivot. It's still a box section aluminium perimeter frame but the frame rails are slim in comparison. It has a very light, fast steering and is particularly adept at quick changes of direction. The current model sports first-class suspension,

included inverted forks, wide wheels with fat radial tyres and some powerful brakes.

This sleek and smart-looking bike is pretty demanding and difficult to ride fast. The motor has to be kept in the upper part of its rev range. The riding position is cramped and offers little in the way of comfort. The ride rewards are high though. There is a lovely sense of smooth rhythm and flow about a GSX-R in full flight on a twisty road. There are no soft edges, everything about the bike is hard and stiff yet sharp and precise. No compromise can be asked for or given. Yet this is what makes a true sportsman's motorbike *par excellence*.

SUZUKI GSX-R1100

JAPAN

ENGINE:
Oil-cooled, DOHC in-line
four

CUBIC CAPACITY:
1127cc

MAXIMUM POWER:
141bhp at 9500rpm

BORE × STROKE:
78 × 59mm

GEARBOX:
five-speed

FINAL DRIVE:
roller chain

WHEELBASE:
1465mm (57.7in)

DRY WEIGHT:
219kg (483lb)

TOP SPEED:
259kph (162mph)

STANDING QUARTER MILE:
10.7sec

DATE OF LAUNCH:
1986

$ SUZUKI

Suzuki's top-of-the-range sports missile, the GSX-R1100 has enjoyed rather a chequered history. It's been around for five years and five different models. While its powerhouse engine has been continually refined and improved, not all of the chassis changes deemed necessary to contain that power have been similarly successful.

Originally designed as a bored and stroked version of the GSX-R750, the mighty 1100 faithfully followed the 750's narrow focus – extreme light weight and huge power with any consideration of ride comfort or ancillary equipment remaining purely secondary. Yet the original 1100 surprised many people in being so different from the 750. A bigger, better bike in every way, its broad and plentiful power coupled with its low weight made other litre-plus bikes of the time appear like lumbering, overweight dinosaurs. Moreover it made the GSX-R750 feel like a fragile toy in comparison. The 1100 was big, sturdy and strong. It found a lot of admirers and friends.

So what went wrong? Well, as ever, the other manufacturers began to catch up. They, too, were offering lighter, more powerful 1000cc-plus bikes and Suzuki started making changes that weren't always for the best.

There's never been a problem with an engine which over the years has proved itself both flexible and reliable. The basic over-square, short stroke, oil cooled and extensively lightened design has never been short of horsepower yet, in 1989, Suzuki chose to increase both bore and stroke, enlarging the capacity from 1052 to 1127cc. At 141hp the bike is restricted in several markets by the fitment of restrictive washers in the exhaust pipes (these can be easily removed). The well-sorted and highly-developed motor likes to rev and its smooth delivery is distinguished by lots of low down poke (helped by short gearing), as well as free-flowing top end power. Above 150mph the 1100 is *still* accelerating, it's not a question of tucking in and clawing back precious mph from the wind. Nor is it a particularly torquey engine. It likes spinning the high numbers on its tachometer.

As the 1100's power increased so did the weight, negating some of its previous advantage. More significantly, when the motor was enlarged to 1127, Suzuki gave it an all-new frame and chassis based on their 750cc factory endurance racer. Wheelbase, rake and trail all diminished, wheel sizes went from 18-inches to 17, wearing fatter tyres, and they made major changes to the front forks. The result was a bike that handled impeccably on the racetrack and at high speed (above 130mph) but wobbled and wandered disconcertingly at road legal speeds. Since most road riders have to do most of their riding well below 130mph the changes couldn't be described as successful. Indeed, quite a few expert riders said the bike was scarey to ride. Most blamed an inadequate front fork.

For 1990 and the latest K model, Suzuki sensibly stretched the wheelbase for stability, added uprated upside-down forks to aid rigidity and fitted much wider tyres – the rear radial is a 180/55-17 on a 5.5in rim. They've also kitted it out with true, full race, multi-adjustable suspension – both front and rear ends are adjustable for spring pre-load, compression and rebound damping and there are thousands of possible combinations. The general complaint now is that there is simply too much choice. Since all suspension functions are inter-related, the ordinary road rider is going to find it very difficult to set up.

Although the newer 1127 versions are undoubtedly superior to the original 1052 models, many enthusiasts prefer the older bike. The current model's sophistication denies a lot of the tuning scope that the original 1100 offered. For example, Suzuki have always been by far the most popular choice among drag racers and many a 1260cc version has been built for drag strip and street use. The best of these have been timed at over 183mph While the doubts continue to linger about the chassis modifications, no such complaints have ever been levelled at the enormous potential of the engine.

JAPAN

ENGINE:
Liquid-cooled, DOHC, in-line four

CUBIC CAPACITY:
749cc

MAXIMUM POWER:
121bhp at 11,500rpm

BORE × STROKE:
72 × 46mm

GEARBOX:
six-speed

FINAL DRIVE:
roller chain

WHEELBASE:
1445mm (56.9in)

DRY WEIGHT:
187kg (412lb)

TOP SPEED:
259kph (162mph)

STANDING QUARTER MILE:
10.9sec

DATE OF LAUNCH:
1989

If this machine looks like a racer, it's because it is! Thinly disguised to make it street legal, removal of the tax disc, number plate, mirrors, indicators and sidestand and fitting some slicks prepares it for the racetrack. Why, then, is it available to the road rider? The reason is relatively simple. The OWO1 was built to compete against Honda's RC30 and Bimota's YB4 in World Superbike racing. In order to campaign a machine in this class certain homologation rules have to be met; these depend on the annual output of motorcycles. If a manufacturer produces more than 100,000 units a year, a minimum of 1,000 of its Superbike contender must be built. Between 50,000 and 100,000, 500 Superbikes are necessary. Small scale manufacturers (like Bimota) only have to build 200 Superbikes to be eligible. In Yamaha's case they have to build 1,000, which means that some go on sale, albeit at huge expense, for road use. They come sparsely equipped for the task.

The OWO1 isn't a road bike, it's a sports-stiff, high-revving, factory racer. As standard, it comes pretty competitively set up for the track. An expensive racekit is available to further hone its fiery performance and turn what's already a lean and purpose-built beast into a real short-fuse, speedball racetrack weapon.

Apart from the wonders of five-valve technology and inclined cylinders, the OWO1 has little in common with the popular FZ750 roadster. Instead it's cobbled together using lessons learnt from the rare and precious YZF750 Genesis, the factory endurance racer, with lots of FZR1000 bits and knowhow thrown in for good and plentiful measure.

The engine is incredibly oversquare and short-stroked. Every part of its assembly is dedicated to getting the biggest and most efficient bangs for your money. It sucks through forward-facing fresh air ducts in the fairing, mixing and feeding the gas through large flat-slide 38mm Mikunis. It has big valves and big, hand-finished ports. Lightweight, short-skirt, stepped-top pistons with large valve cutaways ride on titanium con rods and compress the gas to 11.2:1 (with the racekit this is upped to 13.5 or more). At the same time as it controls ignition timing. Providing a fat spark, an eight-bit microprocessor decides when to activate a servo motor operating a butterfly valve in the collector of the stainless steel four-into-one exhaust system. As on the FZR1000, this exhaust valve (EXUP) compensates for losses in the mid-range that are inevitable in any engine developed for maximum power and torque. The EXUP rotary valve has to close off up to 70 per cent of the exhaust and operate in temperatures of up to 700-degrees C. but it certainly works.

What should be an essentially peaky, sky-high, rev-happy

OPPOSITE, ABOVE AND BELOW:
Yamaha's OWO1 is a sports-stiff, high-revving racer available for road use only because the factory had to build over 1000 examples to homologate it for World Superbike competition. It combines technology from the FZ750, FZR1000 and the YZF factory endurance racer to make for a highly-specialist, narrow-focus sports weapon with more power and performance than any road rider could ever need.

motor is actually endowed with a useful, long flat spread of torque. It can be ridden from 0-5000rpm with fast response and the delivery is crisp, flexible and smooth. It reserves its best power for between 8000 and 13,500rpm, quite a wide range of meaty acceleration. In its stride, it peaks at about 12,000rpm. Translate that through six close-ratio gears into road speed and in top the bike clocks 162mph. A race-kitted version, lighter and more powerful will be tall-geared for over 170mph.

With the cylinders angled forward at 40-degrees (instead of the 45-degrees of the FZ750 road bike), Yamaha's chassis designers took full advantage of the layout and assembled a short, stiff frame, a short wheelbase, fast steering geometry and lots of ground clearance. The deep section aluminium Deltabox frame is obviously rigid and the swing-arm is beautifully crafted. Suspension front and back is by top notch Ohlins units which are multi-adjustable for individual ride preferences. The huge brakes sport Nissan four-piston racing calipers and 320mm discs.

Generally, the bike is very stable on the power, though the steering isn't as quick and nervy as racers typically like. Although the bike is clearly competitive weight-wise, in standard trim it has to be wrestled with, needing a firm grip and a lot of rider input. Naturally, it wouldn't be a racer unless just about every part of its handling performance could be changed to suit the rider. The OWO1 has more power, performance and commitment than the road rider could ever need.

YAMAHA FZR1000

Yamaha's FZR1000 is a maximum sports bike in every sense and has become something of an industry standard. The machine has won countless Bike of the Year awards and has even been voted Best Bike of the Eighties. Its success can largely be attributed to the fact that it does everything pretty well and nothing particularly badly. It has astonishing power yet the chassis can handle it and deliver the performance through the tyres to the road. More significantly, it's comfortable and rider-friendly. Although undeniably a pure sports machine, its abilities are not confined to the racetrack and world-wide sales confirm its position as one of the very best road bikes available.

Developed from the YZF factory endurance racer, the FZR1000 uses much of the engine technology Yamaha first displayed on their pioneering FZ750 road bike. Each of the four cylinders uses five valves – three inlet and two exhaust – and the cylinder bank is inclined forward allowing the use of downdraft carburettors and a short, dead straight inlet path for better cylinder filling.

The result is a free-revving engine that will pull from idling speed to the redline making smooth linear power all the way. Performance is electrifying with instant response anywhere in the wide, flat torque curve and enough brute acceleration to spin the tyre at 90mph.

Performance already assured and restricted to 125hp in a number of markets (carb rubbers blank-off part of the inlet tract and many owners simply take a sharp blade to them), Yamaha unveiled a more powerful version in 1989, the FZR1000 Exup. This made 139hp in unrestricted guise and was equipped with hotter cams, lightweight valvegear and high compression, all in pursuit of more top end poke and speed. To compensate for the slight loss in low and mid-range power, Yamaha fitted an electronic, servo operated rotary valve in the exhaust (Exup). This varied the effective length of the exhaust pipe at different rpm and helped boost low and mid-range power levels.

At the same time, they eased the forward inclination of the cylinders from 45-degrees to 35-degrees, still keeping weight usefully low, forward and bearing on the front wheel but now also enabling them to shorten the wheelbase for faster steering response.

The FZR handles beautifully thanks to the rigidity of the very stiff, large section aluminium frame. Named Deltabox, the frame was developed from Yamaha's vee-four 500cc GP racer and the near vertical position of the FZR's carbs lends itself to peripheral frame layout. Equipped with sturdy forks, well-damped rear suspension and enormous 320mm floating brake discs, the FZR1000 is an object lesson in mating a hugely powerful engine to a strong yet fairly light and fast-responding chassis.

The result is a bike that can be both mannered and monstrous. The flexible power means easy cruising or touring with huge steps in speed is just a flick of the wrist away. Either way, the rider gets a lot of feedback about what's happening on the road. Impressed with the bike's roadholding and stability, confidence increases, he knows he has power available everywhere so gets on the gas harder for a more aggressive ride, pushing the tyres, the suspension and the ground clearance nearer their limit. None of this will faze the FZR. Remarkably consistent in its performance since first launched, Yamaha have chosen not to make any changes since 1989 and many applaud their decision to leave alone what's already been proved a smart and tireless performer.

YAMAHA FJ1200

JAPAN

ENGINE:
Air-cooled, DOHC in-line four

CUBIC CAPACITY:
1188cc

MAXIMUM POWER:
125bhp at 9000rpm

BORE × STROKE:
77 × 63.8mm

GEARBOX:
five-speed

FINAL DRIVE:
roller chain

WHEELBASE:
1490mm (58.7in)

DRY WEIGHT:
238kg (525lb)

TOP SPEED:
243kph (152mph)

STANDING QUARTER MILE:
10.8sec

DATE OF LAUNCH:
1986

The FJ1200 grew out of the FJ1100 which, back in 1984, was the first litre-plus motorcycle to seriously address the problem of all litre-plus motorcycles – how to make something fundamentally big and heavy handle responsively. In both 1100cc and 1200cc form the FJ is a genuine 150mph superbike, combining a huge and immensely strong engine with a low, fairly light-weight chassis. It is a capable and versatile sports-tourer and the 1200 has proved popular worldwide as an all-rounder, a motorcycle for riders looking for a bit of every-thing – comfort, space, load carrying and, perhaps most important, the sort of power and speed that only a big inch engine can produce.

The motor is a compact, slightly inclined, DOHC 16 valve transverse four, remarkable only for the amount of sheer grunt it makes – 125hp at 9000rpm and 80ft/lbs of torque. Output is smooth and strong; a low geared, vibration free, fat torque monster.

This large and heavy lump is unusually mounted. Yamaha realized that weight-saving on a bike this big was futile, so they concentrated on keeping the weight, and indeed the bike, low and compact. Their 'lateral frame concept' was novel in 1984 but is rather more commonplace now. Box-section steel frame rails were the first to laterally hug the sides of the engine rather than conventionally run above it as the top rails of a double cradle. What's still unusual is the way these two main side rails meet ahead of the steering head rather than at it. The steering pivot itself is supported by small-diameter tubes, fully triangulated off the main rails.

The FJ feels low and nimble on the road, hiding its con-siderable wet weight and long wheelbase well. Its most obvious problem is a lack of ground clearance yet, despite its age, everything else about it remains solidly impressive. It can cruise and tour two-up with a mountain of luggage and a high degree of comfort. It can also stomp a seriously twisty road with ability and determination. It's an honest performer with a fully exposed record of exceptional reliability and ruggedness. That air-cooled engine is bulletproof and the cycle is game for anything thrown at it.

Thanks to its sales success Yamaha have kept the FJ vir-tually unchanged since the 1984 1100 and it has remained in their range for longer than they'd originally envisaged. For years it's eaten into BMW's sales as the sports-tourer alternative. Until Honda launched their all-new ST1100 Pan-European in 1990, it had no serious Japanese opposition. It remains in Yamaha's line-up as a trusty old flagship. Its tooling costs long paid for. Its reputation long assured.

OPPOSITE: Essentially unchanged since 1984, Yamaha's FJ1200 sports-tourer is a hugely popular mount thanks largely to its well-rounded, versatile performance. Not only will it haul a huge load in comfort but with the luggage removed, it becomes a nimble and effective sports bike. At the end of 1990, Yamaha became the first of the Japanese manufacturers to offer an ABS anti-lock braking system. The bike they chose to fit it to was the trusty FJ.

YAMAHA V-MAX

JAPAN

ENGINE:
Liquid-cooled, 72 degree,
Vee-4 with Vee-Boost

CUBIC CAPACITY:
1198cc

MAXIMUM POWER:
143bhp at 8500rpm

BORE × STROKE:
76 × 66mm

GEARBOX:
five-speed, constant mesh

FINAL DRIVE:
shaft

WHEELBASE:
1590mm (62.6in)

DRY WEIGHT:
271kg (596lb)

TOP SPEED:
224kph (140mph)

STANDING QUARTER MILE:
10.3sec

DATE OF LAUNCH:
1984

Yamaha's V-Max is designed to excel in the acceleration field. Its top speed of around 140mph is not as high as it might be, given a monstrous Vee-4 engine with a power output of 135bhp, and compared with race-replica models. What is sensational is how quickly it gets to that speed. Acceleration is the V-Max's reason for being, helped by a fat rear tyre like that of a drag bike and gearing to match.

Launched in 1984, the V-Max became at once the ultimate hot rod, the fastest-accelerating road bike ever, sizzling through the standing quarter mile in not quite ten seconds. Ten years before, only specialized dragsters could accelerate like that.

The basis of this factory hot rod was the big Vee-4 engine from Yamaha's 1200cc Venture tourer — a veritable river-barge of a bike, festooned with fairings and luggage gear. All that went, and the V-Max was left behind, spare but still monstrous, its styling dominated by the massive engine with two giant air-scoops for the four down-draught carburettors where you would expect to see the fuel tank. The V-Max, like the Venture, has a low-slung tank beneath the seat, with the fuel pumped up to the four greedy carburettor throats.

A vestigial pillion seat completed the spartan look, while the back tyre behind it was of unprecedented width: a 150/90 × 15 monster.

The engine was revitalized to release more of its fire-breathing potential, with the output rising from 90bhp in Venture trim to a massive 143bhp as the V-Max. The factory hop-up job was thorough, including a stronger crankshaft, lightened pistons with a 10.5:1 compression ratio, bigger valves, and high-lift double overhead camshafts. Yamaha also introduced a novel system of automatic butterfly valves linking the inlet tracts below the carburettors, which smoothed out the power delivery right across the rev range. The V-Max retained the shaft drive of the touring bike, freeing the owner from the burden of replacing shattered rear chains and the hard-worked rear tyre.

In a straight line, there is nothing to touch the V-Max. From a standing start, the way it transmits power instantly to that fat rear tyre leaves all its rivals gasping. If its handling on a twisty road is a bit twitchy, it makes up so much ground *between* the bends that it hardly matters.

On a long high-speed run, the rider — sitting upright and holding onto high and wide handlebars — feels like a parachute as the wind catches the chest. This more or less confined the V-Max's usefulness to the USA, where low speed limits favour fast acceleration at the expense of top speed. Europe did not see the V-Max, except as a spectre of the imagination.

BELOW: Yamaha's V-Max is closely related to movie maniac Mad Max, if only in spirit. Its prime purpose is to cover the quarter-mile in the quickest possible time. To that end, a massively powerful Vee-4 engine crowds the engine bay. Chrome air-scoops are real — what looks like a fuel tank is in reality an air-filter housing. The gas is carried under the seat. The rider hangs on for dear life.

HARLEY-DAVIDSON XLCR

U.S.A.

ENGINE:
Air-cooled, OHV, 45 degree,
Vee-twin

CUBIC CAPACITY:
997.5cc

MAXIMUM POWER:
61bhp at 6200rpm

BORE × STROKE:
81 × 96.8mm

GEARBOX:
four-speed

FINAL DRIVE:
triplex chain

WHEELBASE:
1485mm (58.5in)

DRY WEIGHT:
235kg (520lb)

TOP SPEED:
192 (120mph)

STANDING QUARTER MILE:
13.9sec

DATE OF LAUNCH:
1976

HARLEY-
DAVIDSON

The Harley-Davidson XLCR is known in the heart of every *red-blooded* motorcyclist around the world as a dream café racer – mean, moody, magnificent and *very* black. It is known by many names – Big Black, Black Knight, the Black Brute, Rolling Thunder and plain old XLCR (pronounced Excelsior – how else?) With a black fairing, black cylinders, black cases and black pipes, it looks, sounds and smells like a mighty motorcycle, and it is, caviar on wheels.

Big Black is the fastest production bike Harley-Davidson have ever built. On skyscraper-tall gearing, it hits a good 120mph absolutely flat out. If top speed alone were the criterion for inclusion in this book, no Harley would make the grade. Any current Japanese 250cc machine will knock the pants off it in acceleration, roll-on and top speed tests, but this is to miss the point. The XLCR is about a different kind of power – big vee-twin power with extraordinarily long-stroking thumping explosions. You can count the power pulses at low revs when it rocks rather than vibrates. Two massive 81mm pistons are undertaking a long 96.8mm journey on every stroke and the 9:1 compression ratio helps them on their way with an almighty bang. The XLCR is about a different kind of image – low, massive and mean. Purposeful, powerful, delectable, it is a lean and shadowy beast with a road-shaking 1000cc Vee-twin lump. In fact, the XLCR is no more mythical than a race-modified Sportster 997cc engine in the smaller and lighter frame of Harley's XR750 flat-track racer. That, in conjunction with some stunning looks, is enough to make it the most desirable Harley ever.

At 520lb, it is fairly light for a Harley and it handles adroitly, all things considered. The novel siamesed exhausts give extra power but hardly maximum efficiency. Above all else, the bike has been tailored for looks. The casings are gargantuan and finished in crinkle-black. All of the paintwork and cycle gear is beautifully turned out. Light the fuse and it ticks over lazily but with the most profound bass note any four-stroke has ever produced. At full noise, the exhaust explosions are exquisite: a booming, deafening storm. Lovely. A Harley never barks (maximum torque is at 3800rpm, how could it?) It thumps – and how. Naturally it pulls like a train. The XLCR makes so much torque, it only needs a four-speed gearbox, nicely spaced and with a usefully tall top ratio. Vibration is awful – bad enough to undo the screws retaining major components at up to 80mph, smooth enough up to the ton and definitely on its own anywhere above. In its favour, it is *always* tractable, with power to go a-plenty.

Contradictions and creative legends surround all Harleys

OPPOSITE: **The classic sporting Harley, the XLCR (pronounced Excelsior) was lean, black and thunderous – a throbbing, shaking live animal of a motorcycle. Venerable design kept it below the outer limits of superbike speed but phenomenal low rev and mid-range torque have ensured it a special place in the hall of fame.**

They are exotic, evocative pieces of hardware, essentially unchanged since the dawn of motorcycling and all the better for it. Harley-Davidsons are all things to all people – raw, uncivilized and brutish; classic, owner-accessible and with a plain, no-nonsense image; last of the *real* motorcycles. To say their agricultural engine combines really usable power with good handling would not be enough. Never forget the look, the style, the desperado image and the fact that Harley-Davidson make *the* biggest Vee-twin motorcycles in the world.

Their regular 1340cc Evolution series engines are fitted in a current range of 17 different bikes. None can match the outright speed of the old XLCR, but then the Harley factory abandoned speed-engineering many years ago yet their sales have kept on soaring. Like the people who buy them, Harley-Davidson pursue a different path, a different definition of motorcycle performance.

VANCE & HINES TURBO HONDA

'THE LIVING LEGEND'

U.S.A.

ENGINE:
Air and oil-cooled,
turbocharged, DOHC in line
four

CUBIC CAPACITY:
1140cc

MAXIMUM POWER:
280bhp at 12,500rpm

BORE × STROKE:
74 × 66mm

GEARBOX:
five-speed

FINAL DRIVE:
roller chain

WHEELBASE:
1612mm (63.5in)

DRY WEIGHT:
215kg (474lb)

TOP SPEED:
more than 256kph (160mph)

STANDING QUARTER MILE:
9.9sec

DATE OF LAUNCH:
1969

Mel Mandel's 'Living Legend' Honda is one of the fastest and most famous street bikes in America. It's become a legend in its own life-time largely because Mel bought it as an original 1969 Honday 750/4 and has spent over 20 years developing and transforming it. In that time, man and machine have become virtually inseparable and both have had major surgery. Mel had a serious accident on the Living Legend back in 1987 and had to have his leg rebuilt. The bike was completely rebuilt too.

Just how much '69 Honday is left in Mel's creation is hard to say. The frame is about 75% original but has been strengthened to contain the fabulous amount of horsepower produced by the Vance & Hines turbocharged motor. The original and pioneering Honda 750/4 motor was long ago replaced by a big bore Suzuki GSX1100 lump, lovingly assembled by Byron Hines. Almost every part of the engine and transmission has been micro plated and hard-chromed to reduce friction losses. There is more to this bike than meets the eye. Much more.

Mel, who works as a courier for NBC news crews in Los Angeles, knows only too well that he's built himself a formidable reputation for sheer, straightline speed. The bike has an awful lot of what Mel modestly calls 'passing power'.

'I mind my own business when I ride, but if challenged I turn the real power on. One minute it's just an ordinary '69 Honda going down the road and the next instant it's a 280hp killer street bike.'

'The custom made tank has a split fuel capacity. One side flows junk gas, 92 octane, but if I'm threatened I switch to the other side of the tank which flows 109 octane aviation race gas. The electronically activated air-shifter looks like everyone else's, but I designed the swingarm to accommodate the air reservoir which is fed by an on-board compressor. An electric oil pump feeds the turbo normally but if I want to call up some real boost, I hit the switch that pumps 35lb of oil pressure to the turbo. I switch over the fuel tanks and also turn on the air shifter connected to a centrifugal lock up clutch.'

Mad Mel's message is clear. Don't mess with this bike on the street. It's a wolf in sheep's clothing. At 470lb and making a claimed 280hp (running 27psi of boost on alcohol and high octane race gas) the bike will run 10-second dead, quarter-mile times at 155mph without wheelie bars. And it'll run them easy.

'The whole beauty of the bike in all the years I've owed it,' says Mel, 'is the weight and the horsepower.' He repeats this phrase like a mantra and, though it sounds a little odd, what he means is that for over 20 years he's been pursuing a perfect power to weight ratio. The result is the world's fastest Honda 750/4. It took a team of 25 American specialist firms to build it under Mel's orchestration. Attention to detail, the meticulous design and the high standard of engineering and finish, all stand as testimony to Mel's vision and 20-year-old love affair with this one motorcycle. Nothing is overstated. *Everything* is functional.

Mel likes to joke that he took the loss of his left leg 'in his stride' and that his artificial magnesium and carbon-fibre leg is trickier than the bike. He has plans for updating the bike still further. 'Byron Hines suggested installing a Suzuki two-stage nitrous motor just to keep up with the traffic. It'd be 1150cc housed in a Kosman frame rolling a 10-inch wide rear wheel. It'll be longer but still look the same, with all the metal parts replaced by carbon-fibre. Still a '69 Honda but lighter, with almost double the horsepower. It'll be just a 500hp '69 Honda going down the street just minding its own business but it'll also be a seven-second street bike.'

Mad Mel Mandel and his 'Living Legend' Honda. He's still out there somewhere doing it, shutting down all-comers on a 20-year-old bike. 'If you want to race, that's fine. I've never lost. Nobody's ever been in front of that license plate.'

THE RACERS

CAGIVA V589

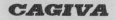
The lone European motor-cycle in 500cc Grand Prix racing is Cagiva's small and striking vee-four. The Italian stallion has now been steadily developed for nearly ten years and is often said to have the greatest potential of all the current 500s. Sadly, however, results to date, indicate it still needs an awful lot of work to make it truly competitive. Despite several top three places, the Cagiva has fallen some way short of ever winning a GP.

To beat the Japanese factories at their own game has been the guiding ambition of the Castiglioni brothers at Cagiva, and if the title could be won on enthusiasm and commitment alone, they would have carried it off years ago.

Originally inspired by Yamaha's early vee-fours, Kenny Roberts helped with the initial testing which first saw the Cagiva line up on a Grand Prix grid. The engine is not a true vee-four, it is really a pair of parallel twins splayed apart in a vee with crankshafts geared together and driving the clutch via an intermediary gear. The angle between the cylinders has changed over the years from 90° to a narrow 56° to today's fairly standard 70° which allows more space for the reed valves and better airflow to the carburettors.

Every season the bike is heavily modified and often radi-cally changed. Before the 1987 season began, the factory approached French designer Alan Chevallier to construct a new lightweight chassis, then abruptly changed their minds and built a wholly new bike in just 30 days, finishing it on the very morning that practice started for the Italian GP. Amaz-ingly, it ran quite well.

For the last few years, Cagiva have struggled against some major problems like excess weight and a lack of top end horsepower. The engine has a lot of mid-range power but little of the brute top end performance that the Japanese factory bikes possess in abundance.

Weight has been shaved by using magnesium crankcases but the Cagiva's extreme forward weight distribution (60/40) and steep steering head angle has led to handling problems. The 1989 twin-spar frame was fabricated in distinctly-grooved, aircraft alloy and is physically stiff but various suspension experiments involving a horizontally-mounted rear shock and a short swingarm have failed to cure the Cagiva's tendency to wheelspin. It steers like a dream but it also lets its tyres break adhesion far too easily.

The Cagiva has enjoyed some successful innovations though. Since 1988 it has used exclusive computerized igni-tion made by Marelli, allowing four different advance curves to be controlled by the rider through a switch at the handle-bars. This unusual facility hints at a full engine management system that Cagiva have been quietly developing for their long-awaited fuel-injected 500 vee-four. In prototype form,

PREVIOUS PAGE: Head down behind the bubble with the throttle wide open, this is Australian Michael Doohan on a 1990 Honda NSR500 Grand Prix racer.

OPPOSITE, ABOVE AND BELOW: One of the most experienced riders in 500cc GP racing, the American Randy Mamola has spent three seasons trying to take the Cagiva V589 to its first GP win. Sadly, the Italian factory announced their withdrawal from GP racing at the end of 1990 though they are still developing a fuel-injected, vee-four 500 for future competition.

the fuel-injected racer has been tested and is reported to be very fast but with unpleasant throttle responses. Doubtless fuel injection is the way to go though and, for once, Cagiva look to be well ahead of the game.

At present, with its beautiful bodywork styled by the Italian master, Massimo Tamburini, the Cagiva is always a welcome and refreshing sight on the track, especially with Randy Mamola aboard. The hugely popular and experienced American rider has a contract with Cagiva containing a clause that rewards him with a Ferrari Tesstarossa should he ever pilot the V589 to its first GP victory. That day still looks some way off. In 1989 at Assen in Holland, Mamola was entertaining the crowd with a few wheelies during the warm-up lap when he flipped the bike over backwards and it never made the starting grid.

HONDA RVF750

JAPAN

ENGINE:
Liquid-cooled, DOHC, 90 degree, Vee-four

CUBIC CAPACITY:
748cc

MAXIMUM POWER:
135 at 12000rpm

BORE × STROKE:
70 × 40.8mm

GEARBOX:
five-speed; constant mesh

FINAL DRIVE:
chain

WHEELBASE:
1402mm (55.2in)

DRY WEIGHT:
152kg (350lb)

TOP SPEED:
more than 280kph (175mph)

DATE OF LAUNCH:
1985

This bike is the most successful four-stroke racer of modern times. When the capacity ceiling for World Endurance and Formula One World Championship racing was changed back in 1984, the RVF won both titles. When the World Superbike Championship was created in 1988, Honda made an expensive, hand-built replica of the RVF750 called the RC30; it was king of the World Superbikes in 1988 and 1989. For good measure, the same bike won the World Formula-One title in the same years. All that success can be directly traced to the original HRC factory endurance racer – the RVF 750, a bike that in its heyday was virtually unbeatable. Now semi-retired and largely replaced by the more common RC30 variations, the factory still wheel out the RVF from time to time. It is raced in long distance 24 hour classics like Le Mans and the Bol d'Or. Honda blow the dust off it and then it proceeds to blow all the competition into the weeds. It is the most competitive and reliable of all race weapons, completely proven and capable of being run flat out for 24 hours, day and night, needing only a regular diet of petrol, oil, tyres, brake pads . . . and riders.

Like the RC30, the RVF is a liquid-cooled, 90-degree, vee-four with gear-driven DOHC, four-valve heads and a 748cc capacity. Almost everything else is completely different and exclusive to the factory racer. The endurance bike makes a maximum of 135hp at 12,000rpm. It uses a rev limiter designed to cut in at 12,500rpm during the six and eight hour races though this is dropped to 12,000rpm for the 24 hour marathons. With a five-speed gearbox and a choice of three possible primary drive ratios, the Honda is geared for a top speed in excess of 175mph. More importantly, the engine produces its power very smoothly with a wide spread of torque. This makes it very tractable, an obvious bonus if the rider has to face typically varied endurance racing weather – sunshine during the day, rain at night and freezing fog at dawn.

The frame, in box-section aluminium, with the engine stressed is very similar to the twin spar frames used by Honda on their 250 and 500cc two-stroke GP racers. Suspension is by Showa all round and at the back there is a very interesting one-sided, aluminium swingarm with an inboard disc and dished wheel. This makes for very quick wheel changes, an essential part of all long distance racing. The 18in rear wheel, wearing a Michelin radial slick, can be changed in under ten seconds flat.

The brakes are fully floating with four piston, Nissan calipers. The dry weight of the bike is 350lb. Since its debut as the official factory racer run under the Honda France banner, the RVF has beaten all-comers and proved immensely

OPPOSITE: Jean-Michel Mattioli on the works RVF during the 1990 Le Mans 24 hour race. His extravagant riding style is unusual in 24 hour racing where above all else it is important not to crash. But Mattioli stayed on board the number one Honda RVF and the legendary Honda France team notched up another marathon victory.

reliable. A competitive endurance bike needs not only speed but also strength. The RVF rarely breaks down. In the expert hands of Endurance World Champions like Alex Viera, Gerard Coudray and Patrick Igoa, it has been crashed only a handful of times over the years and has invariably been patched up quickly and efficiently enough to rejoin the fray.

Endurance racing is an expensive, time consuming and gloriously imaginative affair, an exacting test of both men and machines, passionately supported in Europe and Japan. The equation for success is full of imponderables. Riders need to be hard yet adaptable with a disciplined and well organized pit support crew. Above all a very reliable and plain, quick motorcycle is necessary. The RVF is still the best, a factory racer to be feared whenever and wherever it appears. The bike has emerged over thousands of miles against the 'stop', in all weathers, as the leading contender for major honours. An endurance racer supreme.

JAPAN

ENGINE:
Liquid-cooled, 90-degree, vee-four, two-stroke

CUBIC CAPACITY:
495cc

MAXIMUM POWER:
approx. 160bhp

BORE × STROKE:
54 × 54mm

GEARBOX:
six-speed

FINAL DRIVE:
chain

WHEELBASE:
1375mm (54.2in)

DRY WEIGHT:
128kg (283lb)

TOP SPEED:
more than 288kph (180mph)

DATE OF LAUNCH:
1984

Honda built their vee-four as an answer to Yamaha. But the world's largest motorcycle factory wanted to beat Yamaha, not just copy them. The result is a very different motorcycle, good enough to win the world title in 1985, 1987 and 1989.

The Honda is a true vee-four, all cylinders on a single crankshaft with an angle of 90-degrees between the vee. Especially narrow low-friction bearings have prevented the engine from acquiring excessive width, but it is still wider than any two-crankshaft design. The single-crank Honda engine differs from the twin-crank Yamaha in that the firing order is evenly spaced. The Yamaha always has two pistons firing simultaneously. Honda have produced NSR engines with the crankshaft retimed to emulate this double strike, to see if it would improve mid-range torque; no immediate advantages were found.

There is a great deal of secrecy concerning the engine details. Some things are, however, visible to the onlooker. A set of four 35mm Mikuni flat-slide carburettors within the vee feed the cylinders via crankcase reed valves. The cylinders have five transfer and three exhaust ports with an electronically controlled exhaust power valve operating on all four. There is a multiplate dry clutch, a six-speed gearbox and chain final drive. And almost an embarrassment of horsepower.

When Wayne Gardner won the World Championship in 1987, it was already by far the most powerful motorcycle in 500cc competition. By 1988 though, they'd extracted yet more horsepower from the engine and compressed it into a tiny band at the top of the rev range. The result was virtually unrideable. The bike would light the tyre everywhere. Keeping in the powerband and trying to control the motorcycle proved an almost impossible juggling act. Since 1988, Honda have spent most of their time making the power more amenable and the bike easier to ride.

The frame of this hand-built motorcycle is fairly conventional, a twin-spar design made from rectangular-section aluminium tubing, with a pivoted rear fork operating a rising-rate linkage to the single Showa damper. Carbon-fibre clip-ons and even some carbon-fibre wheels are used as well as carbon-carbon brakes, usually fed by Nissan hydraulics and calipers.

The factory's major achievement with the NSR has been in taming its fearsome character while at the same time making it even faster. When Eddie Lawson won the 1989 world championship on the Honda, he proved he was the best rider in the world, because against all odds, he succeeded in adapting the Honda to his own style after six years of riding for Yamaha.

OPPOSITE, ABOVE: **The Australian Wayne Gardner, the 1987 World Champion who has ridden for Honda throughout his GP career.**

OPPOSITE BELOW: **Mick Doohan, another Australian now in his second season with Honda. Both have had to fight the NSR's brutal power characteristics and endless wheelspin in order to stay on board. Both riders won a GP in 1990.**

Lawson's victory was a rare achievement; the NSR is a rare and precious machine. Every time it pulls up, it is immediately surrounded by as many as six technicians – a tyre man, a rear suspension man, a brake man, a computer anaylist who will check the data from its on-board micro-computer . . . When it is not out on the track, it is normally worked on behind closed doors. Honda have always been very secretive and often unpredictable in their pursuit of the 500cc world title. The NSR perfectly matches their ambition. Secret and powerful.

SUZUKI RGV500

JAPAN

ENGINE:
Liquid-cooled, 60-degree,
vee-four, two-stroke

CUBIC CAPACITY:
498cc

MAXIMUM POWER:
approx. 160bhp

BORE × STROKE:
56 × 50.6mm

GEARBOX:
six-speed

FINAL DRIVE:
chain

WHEELBASE:
1400mm (55.2in)

DRY WEIGHT:
120kg (265lb)

TOP SPEED:
more than 288kph (180mph)

DATE OF LAUNCH:
1987

Suzuki have not won the 500cc world championship since 1982 when the factory racer was the RG500, a square-four and one of the longest-lived racing engines of modern times. The RG500 took part in the dawn of two-stroke domination of the top 500cc class of road racing and wrote its name large in the record books. The square-four took Barry Sheene to two world championships in the late 1970s and in its heyday took the manufacturer's championship for seven consecutive seasons.

The RG was officially retired at the end of 1986 when it became clear that a lack of power, compared with the more recently designed Yamaha and Honda Vee 4 engines, was keeping the bike out of the top results. Suzuki took up the challenge once again in 1987 with their own Vee 4, the RGV500, and it is this bike that has been steadily developed and refined since. It is not easy to build and campaign a new bike in the fierce competition of modern 500cc Grand Prix racing, but Suzuki have made good progress with the RGV and have won a number of races without ever quite sustaining the effort over a full season and thereby taking the world title. The 56 × 50.6mm twin-crank Vee 4 started life as a clone of a somewhat old-fashioned Yamaha but took a major step forward for the 1989 season. Like the current Yamahas, the crankshafts are geared directly together, so they rotate in opposite directions. As well as eliminating torque reaction, this has allowed a more compact engine, and Suzuki have taken greater advantage of this than Yamaha, by building the trimmest-looking 500 Vee 4 of them all.

Suzuki's engine has never been the most powerful but good mid-range performance and overall light weight has meant that it accelerates fast enough. Its biggest asset is handling, especially the ability to turn quickly going into corners and midway through them. The quick handling has been achieved by taking weight off the front wheel and shifting the compact engine rearwards in the frame. This is against conventional wisdom but works for the RGV since the designers also moved the engine downwards making the centre of gravity lower.

Generally acknowledged as the best-handling GP 500 bike, the RGV has a twin-spar fabricated box-section aluminium frame fashioned in the Deltabox style. The inverted front forks are by Kayaba. Rear rocker arm suspension feeds a multi-adjustable, single Kayaba unit. Various front wheel sizes have been tried, including 16 and 17in, and the Suzuki has consistently used AP Lockheed carbon brake discs.

The result is a nimble and often highly effective machine particularly in the hands of Kevin Schwantz, the flamboyant Texan rider who won six Grand Prix races and occupied

OPPOSITE: Same bike, same rider, different sponsors. In 1989 the Suzuki RGV was sponsored by Pepsi. In 1990 it became the Lucky Strike Suzuki. In both seasons, the hugely talented American, Kevin Schwantz won numerous GPs and was favourite to become 500cc World Champion but he crashed far too often and other more consistent riders stole the crown.

nine pole positions during the 1989 season. But the Suzuki also had the worst reliability record among the Japanese bikes, which seldom breakdown. The RGV suffered ignition, crankshaft and piston failures, which some felt was the result of reducing size and weight a bit too much. The intense development of the Suzuki goes on, though, and the RGV looks likely to win a world title sooner rather than later.

JAPAN

ENGINE:
Liquid-cooled, 70-degree, vee-four, two-stroke

CUBIC CAPACITY:
498cc

MAXIMUM POWER:
approx. 160bhp

BORE × STROKE:
56 × 50.6mm

GEARBOX:
six-speed

FINAL DRIVE:
chain

WHEELBASE:
1381mm (54.4in)

DRY WEIGHT:
131kg (289lb)

TOP SPEED:
more than 288kph (180mph)

DATE OF LAUNCH:
1982

A Grand Prix motorcycle is designed for only one purpose . . . to get past the chequered flag first after some 75 miles of racing. To do this, it needs to be very fast, but that is not all. It must also have good brakes, agile roadholding and reliability. It is this combination which produces a winner.

Yamaha's YZR500 is an exemplary racing motorcycle. Winner of the world championship for rider Eddie Lawson in 1984, 1986 and 1988, the bike is not only fast but is reliable enough to have completed more than three consecutive seasons without a single breakdown. With the high stress engineering inseparable from ultimate performance, that is an achievement indeed.

YZR500 is a generic name covering several generations of Yamaha racers. The YZR in question is the latest version, the Vee-4, that began life as the OW61. Although the latest bike is much changed in detail, the fundamental design has remained much the same.

The engine is not a true Vee-4. Two separate pairs of oversquare cylinders are arranged in a vee, but each has its own crankshaft which is geared together to drive the multi-plate dry clutch. Perhaps it should be called a W4. In this it follows Yamaha's long-established racing pattern, and can trace its ancestry back to the YZR500 in-line four. This also had two crankshafts, placed end to end; the following square four had the pairs of cylinders one behind the other. They were rearranged in a vee (or a W) in 1983, for Kenny Roberts' last Grand Prix year.

In this form, the engine used disc valves cleverly arranged and bevel-driven within the vee between the cylinders to control induction. Turning at half-engine speed, each valve served two cylinders. In 1984, Yamaha followed Honda's lead in introducing reed-valve induction. Employed primarily to make the bike start more quickly in the old dead-engine, Grand Prix push starts. Crankcase reed-valve induction is still used today even though the races now have clutch starts with engines running. With six transfer and three exhaust ports, the YZR also uses an electronically controlled cylindrical valve varying exhaust port height. A six-speed gearbox is behind the engine, and final drive is by chain, just like a road bike.

The Yamaha frame is an exercise in robust lightweight construction. Fabricated from sheet aluminium it takes the form of a twin-spar structure. Front suspension is by telescopic forks with multi-adjustable damping. The anti-dive mechanism was removed in 1985 as it offered no positive benefits on a race track. The rear pivoted fork is also strongly constructed from lightweight aluminium, and operates a rising-rate linkage to compress the single Ohlins damper.

World Champions, old and new.
OPPOSITE BELOW: **The American Eddie Lawson, four times 500cc World Champion.**

OPPOSITE ABOVE: **For 1990 his team-mate was the American Wayne Rainey whose consistency won him the world title and the manufacturer's championship for Yamaha.**

Power has risen through the years until it is now more than 160 brake horsepower – enough to give the bike blinding acceleration and a top speed in the region of 190mph. In 1989, Yamaha pioneered the use of on-board computerized data acquisition. A small computer is programmed to record almost any aspect of performance and behaviour – suspension, chassis flex, power curves, throttle opening and response, carburettor settings, airbox pressure – anything capable of measurement can be recorded and analyzed. This has greatly helped development and enhanced still further the Yamaha's formidable reputation for reliability.

SUPERBIKING POWERHOUSE

It was once the aim of the racing engine designer to achieve 100 horsepower for every litre of capacity. He was prepared to make all kinds of sacrifices to achieve this – an engine that would not idle, that was hard to start, and that used as much fuel as it liked. Power was the main consideration.

Modern motorcycle engines have made a nonsense of those figures. It is a poor machine that does not better 100bhp/litre. The achievement today is to make an engine that is quiet, clean and as polite as a country cleric's runabout, yet capable of revving like a race bike, and of doing it almost indefinitely.

The modern superbike would have reached its current stage of development without the computer, but it would have taken much longer. Computer design techniques offer not only the facility for rapid and comprehensive calculation, but also the chance to perform simulations of both frame and engine design variations without cutting or casting any metal. In the end there is no substitute for bench- or road-testing, but today many variations can be tried and many corners cut on the way.

In the engine

Four new techniques in motorcycle engines deliver the goods now and promise more improvement in the future.

The first is the oil-cooling system developed by Suzuki for their GSX-R750 and 1100 models; the second is the electronic engine management equipment used by BMW and Kawasaki for their top models; the third is the swirl-promoting combustion chambers common to many engines; and the fourth applies only to two-strokes – the variable exhaust geometry that has radically improved the spread of power without impairing the ultimate quantity at high revs.

The prime benefit of Suzuki's oil cooling is in reduction of engine weight. The four-cylinder units carry the same amount of metal as a conventional finned and air-cooled machine, yet offer the close temperature control of liquid-cooled engines *without* carrying all the extra weight of water-jackets, pipes and radiators, not to mention the coolant itself.

It can be argued that all engines are oil-cooled. Circulation of the lubricant, especially over the cylinder heads, inevitably removes heat from the hot spots, and redistributes it to colder parts of the engine. Suzuki's trick (and it is not a new technique, originally dating back to the 1930s) is to reinforce this property by deliberate design. Their engine not only carries extra oil, but also a second oil-circulating system, supplementing the high-pressure lubrication, and devoted purely to washing oil over the hot spots in liberal quantities.

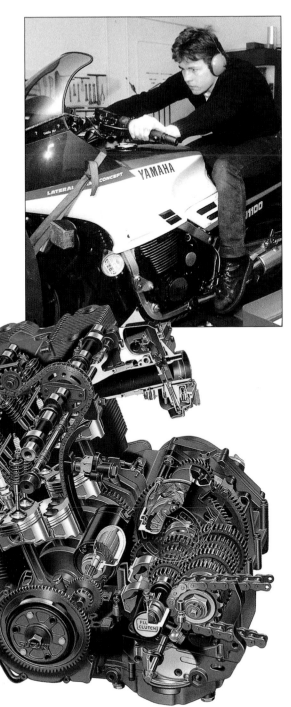

Remove the camshaft covers and it is plain to see how a cascade of oil is directed over the cylinder heads, especially in the area of the exhaust ports, the hottest part of the engine. The oil runs back to the sump by gravity and then is pumped through a radiator to shed its heat.

Good cooling allows an engine with closer tolerances. It improves longevity and full-throttle stamina and allows for higher tuning with less risk. Suzuki have achieved all these benefits without the weight and complication of a separate external cooling system, and it paid instant dividends on road and racetrack.

Electronic engine management was introduced in a limited form by Kawasaki and brought to the next level by BMW. Two areas are affected, ignition and fuel supply, and the more sophisticated system integrates the two so that just one 'brain' does it all.

Computer-controlled electronic ignition is nothing new. Electronic sensors take the place of mechanical contact-breaker points to measure crankshaft rotation, and specifically the point where the sparking plug is triggered to fire (some time before the piston reaches top dead centre, to allow for combustion delays). Simultaneously, the 'brain' is informed at what speed the engine is turning, and the amount of throttle opening (via the inlet manifold vacuum).

Pre-programmed circuits then impose secondary instructions that override the trigger, to advance the timing as revs rise, or to retard it to make the engine easier to start, with all sorts of shades in between.

The timing of the spark is not only exact, but can be tailored to the characteristics of an individual engine design. The system is also amenable to the introduction of a rev-limiter, which kills the sparks to avoid engine damage after a missed gearchange, for example.

Computerized control of the fuel mixture is more complex, and is a process in which carburettors can play no part. It is essential to have electronic fuel injection.

RIGHT: BMW's K-series models introduced integrated electronic engine management, with computers controlling ignition and fuel injection.

OPPOSITE ABOVE LEFT: The fuel injection replaces carburettors with compact and simple-looking tubes and everything is precisely metered.

OPPOSITE ABOVE RIGHT: Much more traditional but highly effective – Yamaha's FZR1000 has the cylinder bank inclined forwards allowing the use of downdraft carburettors with a short, straight inlet path. The near vertical position of the carbs lends itself to peripheral frame layout. Here it is Yamaha's large section aluminium Deltabox frame.

The timing of the spurt of fuel injected is fixed; what varies is the duration (and hence the quantity) of the moment of injection. The parameters are more complex than for ignition. In the case of the BMW, ambient and coolant temperature, the speed of the intake air and the engine speed are all measured, and the Bosch control computer is also linked with the ignition control computer. Thus each individual spurt of fuel is precisely timed and controlled to match exactly the engine's requirements for that particular power stroke – a big advance over the hit-or-miss nature of a carburettor.

The benefits are immediately obvious – easy starting and better fuel economy. The cleaner exhaust gases are harder to measure. Electronic engine management is likely to become more common in the near future.

Not so turbo-charging, which enjoyed a brief vogue, but never achieved the popularity on two wheels that it has on four. The main reason for this is inherent in the nature of the system.

Turbo-charging uses the energy of gases escaping down the exhaust pipe to spin a turbine, which is in turn connected to another turbine which pressurizes the intake system, packing in more fuel/air mixture in the same way as the classic supercharger.

BELOW: The goal is super-speed, and privately modified bikes like this 1100cc Kawasaki and 1138cc Suzuki each have turbochargers and nitrous oxide injection – note the laughing gas bottles strapped on the rear.

If the exhaust pressure is low, with the engine at low revs or small throttle openings, the turbo-charger consequently turns very slowly or not at all. It needs the engine to be driving hard before it can reach working speed (in excess of 20,000rpm), and make it drive harder still.

Motorcycles use relatively small engines, exhaling small amounts of gas. Most existing turbo-chargers were simply too large to work at anything except the very highest revs. Thus fitment to a motorcycle engine imposed sluggish response and a delay in answering the throttle in the engine's most common working rev range – the dreaded turbo lag. They only started to yield benefits when the motorcycle was already going fast.

Even so, all four Japanese manufacturers offered turbo-charged models. Honda's in particular was a masterpiece of complexity, attempting to overcome the turbo's disadvantages with a full house of electronic engine controls. However, the CX500 Turbo performed little beter than a normally aspirated 750 model, was heavier, more expensive, and the throttle response was worse. Motorcycles do not need turbo-chargers. If you are short of power buy a model with a bigger engine.

There is another system that gives a spurt of extra power on demand, with no delays. It is nitrous oxide injection . . . laughing gas. Simply, a pressure bottle of gas is fitted to the motorcycle and plumbed into the intake system. Press a button on the handlebars and the gas enters the combustion

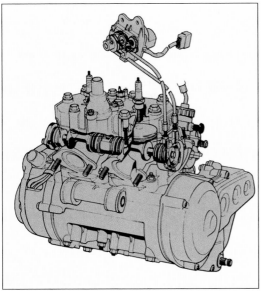

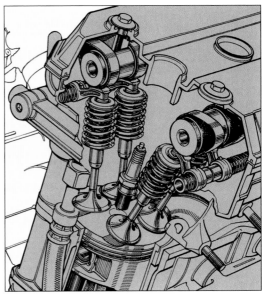

chamber where it breaks down in the combustion process to release oxygen. The only other component that is necessary is an extra spurt of petrol to go in with it, and it has the same effect as instant supercharging.

No production bike has ever been fitted with nitrous oxide injection, but it can be bought as an accessory. Simple to install, devastating in its results, the only drawback is the short-term effect . . . and that you quickly use up the amount of gas that it is convenient to carry. For guaranteed results, adding as much as 50 per cent to your power output in a split second, there is nothing quite like laughing gas.

The factories rely on more subtle effects to improve performance. The third item in our quartet of stars of modern engineering is improved combustion by swirl induction. This means that the fuel/air mixture enters the combustion chamber in a turbulent state, like so many eddies and whirlpools. When the sparking plug sets it on fire, the turbulence spreads the flame front quickly through the entire chamber. Combustion is faster, more complete, and more efficient – leading to more power and better economy.

There are several different ways of doing this, many with acronymic titles. YICS (Yamaha intake controlled swirl) is a system that links intake ports with angled high-velocity tubes, while Suzuki's TSCC (twin swirl combustion chamber) is a four-valve system that feeds a pair of linked chambers within each head.

The most technically complex is Yamaha's latest cylinder head, with an unprecedented *five* valves. Two serve the exhaust, another two the inlet. The fifth is an ancillary inlet valve shooting an extra jet of mixture in at an angle to the main flow.

Finally – two-strokes. Here recent advances have concentrated on the exhaust geometry. The back-pressure of the exhaust is vital to improve the compression of the engine, since the port remains open after the cylinder has filled with mixture and has begun compression. Modern tuning techniques use the harmonics of the exhaust's resonance to send pressure waves back to 'close' the port before the piston has done so. The problem is that the harmonics remain constant but the revs rise and fall, so the harmonic that suits full power at high revs may be quite wrong over the rest of the engine's range, severely damaging performance and fuel efficiency. Designers cope with this by changing the geometry of the exhaust system in various ingenious ways.

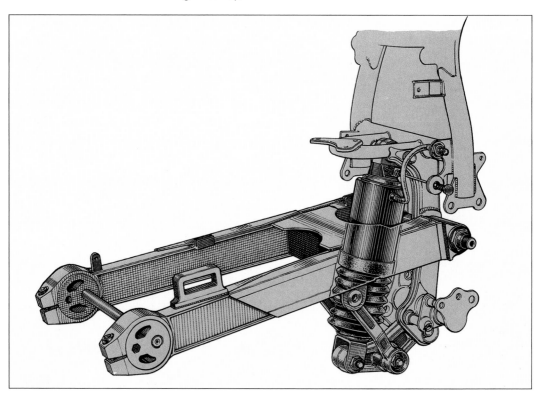

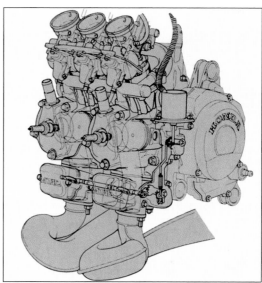

The YPVS (Yamaha power valve system) changes the timing of the port itself. A rotating barrel valve at the top of the exhaust port is closed at low revs, giving mild timing and good bottom-end power. As the revs rise, it gradually opens to advance the port timing. This suits the faster gas flow and allows the two-stroke engine to deliver its full potential power at the top end, yet to start easily and behave well when trickling through the traffic.

Honda developed a different approach, dubbed ATAC, which leaves the port undisturbed but varies the volume of the resonating exhaust expansion chamber, thus changing the frequency of its harmonic pressure pulses. A valve on the exhaust pipe opens at low revs so that an ancillary exhaust chamber is plumbed in to the system. At high revs, the valve snaps shut, leaving the carefully profiled expansion chamber to do its job alone. Suzuki use a similar system with a smaller ancillary chamber that is cast into the cylinder barrel.

These techniques have transformed two-strokes, making their exhausts burn cleaner and improving fuel economy and rideability.

Frame tricks

Better engine performance could be a liability if the chassis is not good enough. The latest superbikes have developed fast in recent years to ensure that road-holding matches speed potential.

The first revolution has been in materials. Traditional drawn steel tubes have in many cases given way to aluminium – a simple and effective way of saving weight.

Designs have also evolved, particularly in relation to the rigid fixing of the steering head (flex in this area inevitably leads to wayward roadholding). The main development has been to escape from the legacy of the bicycle where the steering head is at the end of tubing in a single plane. Motorcycles have long used twin-cradle frames, so that it is at the apex of a triangle.

More recently, spurred by the Italian specialist builders Bimota, the frame has been extended forward of the steering head, so that it can be affixed from all sides. Another technique is to increase radically the angle included by the frame tubes, so that the frame tubes are now wider than the engine, passing on the outside of it rather than over the top. Examples of these perimeter or twin-spar beam frames are now numerous.

The biggest advances have been concerned with rear suspension. Traditionally a pivoted fork was sprung by a pair of spring/damper units, one on each side. It was Yamaha who first replaced this with a single unit, operated by a cantilevered triangulated structure, which was their monoshock derived from a much earlier system developed in Britain by Vincent-HRD.

The recent revolution has been to interpose a geometrically sophisticated system of links between the trailing

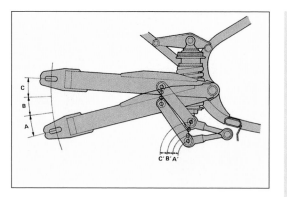

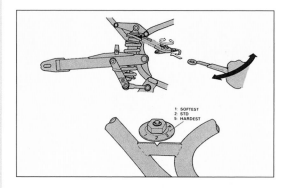

pivoted fork and the spring. By careful arrangement of the bell-cranks and levers, a rising rate can be achieved easily.

This means that the middle portion of the wheel movement compresses the spring relatively less than it does as the suspension reaches its limits. In effect, the ride is soft and comfortable under normal circumstances. Hit a larger bump (or load the suspension more, as in hard cornering), and it stiffens up progressively, giving a firmer ride and more accurate roadholding. Recent developments mean the rider can adjust rear spring preload, compression and rebound damping.

No other single design feature has brought a bigger improvement in motorcycle roadholding. But that's not the only advantage; in addition, it has considerably improved comfort in the process – reconciling two previously mutually exclusive areas of performance.

The motorcycle may still show its ancestral links with the bicycle, but it is difficult to believe when riding a modern superbike.

BIKES OF THE FUTURE

It shows an unrealistic lack of respect for the motorcycles of the present to suggest that those of the near future will be significantly different.

True, the current designs still show strong links with their bicycle ancestors, both in the use of tubular frames and in their steering geometry with a high steering axis and a long front fork. It is possible to criticize them as fundamentally ill-suited to the prersent-day tasks of carrying heavy engines that produce more than 100 horsepower. At the same time, there is no denying that these anachronistic over-powered sprung bicycles do a remarkably efficient job, and that the superbikes of the 1980s have improved rapidly and con-siderably compared with those of the previous decade.

The same rate of progress would see the motorcyclist of the 1990s riding a lighter machine, with a 750cc engine (or perhaps a supercharged 500) producing the same sort of torque and horsepower as the swiftest 1000cc machines in this book.

The frame will probably be a simple spine-type structure in steel or aluminium; the rear pivoted fork of similar struc-ture. The front and rear suspension – far from being the interlinked pneumatic radial arms of the imagination, and in spite of a number of attractive existing alternatives – will be telescopic front forks, with a rising-rate-linkage monoshock at the rear. Unless . . .

What if things had been different from the start? What if the bicycle had never been invented? What if the motorcycle had been conceived by a car designer, fed up with the excess weight and width of his four-wheeled tin box and desirous of some *real* high performance as well as the ability to use it? (Indeed, Gottlieb Daimler's first 'car' of 1885 was more of a motorcycle, with a pair of outrigger wheels.)

The first question the designer would ask himself is how he would sit in this new contraption. Lying on his stomach? Reclining as in a hammock? Both would be possible, but probably not as attractive as something already familiar to him; to ride it like a horse. The engine naturally falls between his knees and feet, and he is straddling the mechanical beast.

Considering the speeds the designer is contemplating, and his background in cars, he will certainly insist on at least as much protection from wind and weather as in an open sports car. He might even like the idea of being strapped into a safety capsule with a roof, with penumatic balancing legs kicking out automatically to balance the machine at rest (he might even favour a gyroscope, operat-ing at very low speeds to hold the machine vertical . . . useful for parking as well as stopping at the lights).

However, since he seems to be a sporting, outdoor type, he will probably stay with his preconceptions of the horse,

ABOVE LEFT: Malcolm Newell's Phasar, a feet-forward motorcycle in which the rider reclines as if in a hammock. The Z1300 six cylinder engine combined with the open cockpit and streamlined bodywork gave it astonishing speed.

ABOVE RIGHT: The classic cigar shape of a land speed record bike. This is Colin Wilson's Project 240,22ft long but surprisingly light at 650lb. The bike was later renamed Project 360 and its aim is to better Don Vesco's 1978 land speed record of 318mph.

OPPOSITE ABOVE: The Foale QL looks bulky, but is exeptionally light. Under its carbon fibre bodywork lies a sparse frame and wishbone suspension.

OPPOSITE BELOW: Engima variation. The later Foale Q2 was built for *Superbike Magazine* and powered by a Suzuki GSX1100 engine.

and choose to sit outside of the main bodywork (though behind a comprehensive and aerodynamic fairing) and to wear protective clothes to beat the weather. As with the horse it is better, if you fall off, to be well clear of the beast, so there would be no question of safety belts.

Having organized the distribution of motorcycle and rider, and allowed for a modicum of secure luggage stowage space, the designer will turn to the construction. His car background will tell him to make the bodywork and the chassis in a single complex structure, a monocoque. Pressed steel would be the chosen material, or would be if he was planning to build a large number. For this first prototype, though, or for a small production run, he will construct it of welded tubes, and the bodywork of moulded glass- and carbon-fibre. The frame will hug the engine, coming in close ahead and behind. This is in order to provide location for the suspension pivots.

It is absolutely certain that an engineer with a clean sheet of paper would not choose to design telescopic forks. Instead, he would probably look at car front suspensions and soon decide that the best alternative was a double-wishbone set-up, with the steering axis in the centre of the wheel. This could follow racing car practice but with the wheel 'upright' pivoted at each end in line with the wheel centre. It could be placed above the wheel, with both ends within a dished wheel, or even straddling these two points via an arced upright.

Common sense and design economy would dictate feeding the suspension loads in as close to the centre of the structure as possible. Instead of a long frame running alongside the front wheel, with the wishbones sideways to it, as in a car, he would turn the design through 90 degrees so that they pointed forwards, and were pivoted on the frame ahead of the engine. They would then need to be arced, to bypass the wheel on full steering lock. Thus the wheel would be unencumbered on one side, with a pair of wishbones modified into C-shaped leading arms on the other.

For the rear suspension, a single trailing arm would suffice, containing the shaft drive. A single suspension unit would be operated by a linkage, to provide a rising rate: comfortable at first, and firming up progressively as it was compressed.

The bike would be steered by a pair of levers, held like the handles of a revolver. As the feet would be needed to balance the machine, these levers would have to incorporate controls for the clutch, accelerator, brakes, and starter (just in case of stalling at a red light).

The seat would be arranged above the frame, and the bodywork would allow free access to it, while shielding the rider from the high-speed blast of air and weather. Naturally, it would be designed for the optimum aerodynamic penetration, as well as to aid stability at high speed by providing some downforce.

With all this the designer would be ready to show the rest of the world in their cars a thing or two about acceleration and agility. The finished machine would look a cross between a bullet and a modern superbike, in spite of being fundamentally different in its evolutionary starting point. While the Japanese churn out bicycle-replicas by the hundreds of thousands, a handful of creative engineers are exploring ideas very similar to these. It is anything but far fetched.

True to its reputation for amiable eccentricity, Great Britain is a natural home to these people. It was in Britain in the 1970s that the first motorcycle with a roof was sold to the public. The Quasar offered a number of radically new alternatives all in one – the roof, so to speak, capping them all. The Quasar was the most successful of a breed of motorcycle called 'Feet Forward', in which the rider reclines in something resembling a hammock. With a body shaped like an arrow, it used a tubular frame with Earle's type fork front suspension. Though it cruised economically and rapidly, its drawback was a pedestrian 750cc Reliant car engine that left it breathless compared with the power of a real superbike.

Later, the same designer, Malcolm Newell, remedied this. His Phasar used a twin-cam Kawasaki Z1300 engine, and had an open cockpit, like a World War One fighter. With its small frontal area and streamlined bodywork it could reach 130mph with astonishing acceleration.

In the meantime, others were exploring wishbone suspension. A racer called Norman Hossack, late of Maclaren

car Formula-One racing team, put the wishbones above the wheel, with what looked like old-fashioned 'girder' forks in fact performing the role of an extended wheel upright.

In another small workshop, long-time front-fork iconoclast Tony Foale was developing a different wishbone-type arrangement, which was radical also in that it disposed by example of a number of the sacred cows of motorcycle geometry. The lower wishbone on his QL (Quantum Leap) was C-shaped, and curved in to the centre of the wheel. The upright rose to above the centre of the tyre, where the top wishbone provided location.

ABOVE AND ABOVE RIGHT:
Bimota's 'Tesi' uses all-new design
with leading-arm front suspension
that looks simple but is surprisingly
complex.
OPPOSITE RIGHT: Hossack design
offers wishbone suspension to fit
onto a conventional bike frame.

Simultaneously, in France, ex-Renault Formula-One designers were working along similar lines to build a radical Grand Prix racing machine. Known as the Elf, after its sponsors this made arcs out of both wishbones, with the upright within the deeply dished wheel. An endurance racing version appeared promising but unreliable at a few Le Mans 24-hour races, and when the Grand Prix version appeared in 1985 it plainly required more development before it could challenge the existing order of telescopic-forked machines from Honda, Yamaha and Suzuki.

There is enough appeal in the idea to attract others in Europe as well. The Italian firm Bimota, already famous for improving on the existing type of frame structure, are among those researching new designs. They are developing the Tesi (Theory), using a single leading arm up front to provide hub-centre steering, with the steering transmitted hydraulically.

The biggest possible sign that the days of the telescopic fork may be numbered came at the 1985 Tokyo Motor Show. There, Suzuki showed the Falcorustyco, stunning not so much for its hub-centre steering and revolutionary styling (which had already been seen in Europe), but for the fact that it was shown by one of the major Japanese manufacturers. Until now, although innovative in detail and in engine design, they have remained conservative in matters of fundamental approach, and since, by force of sales strength, it is the Japanese who dictate the direction of the market, this may be a very significant motorcycle indeed.

THE RECORD
BREAKERS

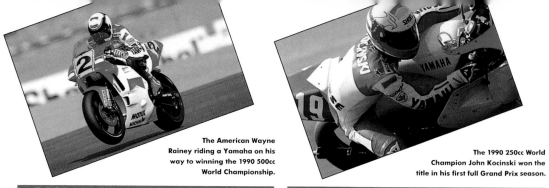

The American Wayne Rainey riding a Yamaha on his way to winning the 1990 500cc World Championship.

The 1990 250cc World Champion John Kocinski won the title in his first full Grand Prix season.

PAST 500CC WORLD CHAMPIONS

YEAR	RIDER	MANUFACTURER
1949	Leslie Graham (British, AJS)	AJS
1950	Umberto Masetti (Italian, Gilera)	Gilera
1951	Geoff Duke (British, Norton)	Norton
1952	Umberto Masetti (Italian, Gilera)	Gilera
1953	Geoff Duke (British, Gilera)	Gilera
1954	Geoff Duke (British, Gilera)	Gilera
1955	Geoff Duke (British, Gilera)	Gilera
1956	John Surtees (British, MV Agusta)	MV Agusta
1957	Libero Liberati (Italian, Gilera)	Gilera
1958	John Surtees (British, MV Agusta)	MV Agusta
1959	John Surtees (British, MV Agusta)	MV Agusta
1960	John Surtees (British, MV Agusta)	MV Agusta
1961	Gary Hocking (Rhodesian, MV Augusta)	MV Agusta
1962	Mike Hailwood (British, MV Agusta)	MV Agusta
1963	Mike Hailwood (British, MV Agusta)	MV Agusta
1964	Mike Hailwood (British, MV Agusta)	MV Agusta
1965	Mike Hailwood (British, MV Agusta)	MV Agusta
1966	Giacomo Agostini (Italian, MV Agusta)	MV Agusta
1967	Giacomo Agostini (Italian, MV Agusta)	MV Agusta
1968	Giacomo Agostini (Italian, MV Agusta)	MV Agusta
1969	Giacomo Agostini (Italian, MV Agusta)	MV Agusta
1970	Giacomo Agostini (Italian, MV Agusta)	MV Agusta
1971	Giacomo Agostini (Italian, MV Agusta)	MV Agusta
1972	Giacomo Agostini (Italian, MV Agusta)	MV Agusta
1973	Phil Read (British, MV Agusta)	MV Agusta
1974	Phil Read (British, MV Agusta)	MV Agusta
1975	Giacomo Agostini (Italian, Yamaha)	Yamaha
1976	Barry Sheene (British, Suzuki)	Suzuki
1977	Barry Sheene (British, Suzuki)	Suzuki
1978	Kenny Roberts (American, Yamaha)	Yamaha
1979	Kenny Roberts (American, Yamaha)	Yamaha
1980	Kenny Roberts (American, Yamaha)	Yamaha
1981	Marco Lucchinelli (Italian, Suzuki)	Suzuki
1982	Franco Uncini (Italian, Suzuki)	Suzuki
1983	Freddie Spencer (American, Honda)	Honda
1984	Eddie Lawson (American, Yamaha)	Yamaha
1985	Freddie Spencer (American, Honda)	Honda
1986	Eddie Lawson (American, Yamaha)	Yamaha
1987	Wayne Gardner (Australian, Honda)	Honda
1988	Eddie Lawson (American, Yamaha)	Yamaha
1989	Eddie Lawson (American, Honda)	Honda
1990	Wayne Rainey (American, Yamaha)	Yamaha

PAST 250CC WORLD CHAMPIONS

YEAR	RIDER	MANUFACTURER
1949	Bruno Ruffo (Italian, Moto Guzzi)	Moto Guzzi
1950	Dario Ambrosini (Italian, Benelli)	Benelli
1951	Bruno Ruffo (Italian, Moto Guzzi)	Moto Guzzi
1952	Enrico Lorenzetti (Italian, Moto Guzzi)	Moto Guzzi
1953	Werner Haas (West German, NSU)	NSU
1954	Werner Haas (West German, NSU)	NSU
1955	Hermann Müller (West German, NSU)	NSU
1956	Carlo Ubbiali (Italian, MV Agusta)	MV Agusta
1957	Cecil Sandford (British, Mondial)	Mondial
1958	Tarquinio Provini (Italian, MV Agusta)	MV Agusta
1959	Carlo Ubbiali (Italian, MV Agusta)	MV Agusta
1960	Carlo Ubbiali (Italian, MV Agusta)	MV Agusta
1961	Mike Hailwood (British, Honda)	Honda
1962	Jim Redman (Rhodesian, Honda)	Honda
1963	Jim Redman (Rhodesian, Honda)	Honda
1964	Phil Read (British, Yamaha)	Yamaha
1965	Phil Read (British, Yamaha)	Yamaha
1966	Mike Hailwood (British, Honda)	Honda
1967	Mike Hailwood (British, Honda)	Honda
1968	Phil Read (British, Yamaha)	Yamaha
1969	Kel Carruthers (Australian, Benelli)	Benelli
1970	Rod Gould (British, Yamaha)	Yamaha
1971	Phil Read (British, Yamaha)	Yamaha
1972	Jarno Saarinen (Finnish, Yamaha)	Yamaha
1973	Dieter Braun (West German, Yamaha)	Yamaha
1974	Walter Villa (Italian, Harley-Davidson)	Harley-Davidson
1975	Walter Villa (Italian, Harley-Davidson)	Harley-Davidson
1976	Walter Villa (Italian, Harley-Davidson)	Harley-Davidson
1977	Mario Lega (Italian, Morbidelli)	Morbidelli
1978	Kork Ballington (South African, Kawasaki)	Kawasaki
1979	Kork Ballington (South African, Kawasaki)	Kawasaki
1980	Anton Mang (West German, Kawasaki)	Kawasaki
1981	Anton Mang (West German, Kawasaki)	Kawasaki
1982	Jean-Louis Tournadre (French, Yamaha)	Yamaha
1983	Carlos Lavado (Venezuelan, Yamaha)	Yamaha
1984	Christian Sarron (French, Yamaha)	Yamaha
1985	Freddie Spencer (American, Honda)	Honda
1986	Carlos Lavardo (Venezuelan, Yamaha)	Yamaha
1987	Anton Mang (West German, Honda)	Honda
1988	Alfonso Pons (Spanish, Honda)	Honda
1989	Alfonso Pons (Spanish, Honda)	Honda
1990	John Kocinski (American, Yamaha)	Yamaha

The youngest World Champion ever, Italian Loris Capirossi was just 17 when he won his first 125cc Grand Prix and the World title.

The experienced crew of Alain Michel and Simon Birchall are the 1990 Sidecar World Champions.

PAST 125CC WORLD CHAMPIONS

YEAR	RIDER	MANUFACTURER
1949	Nello Pagani (Italian, Mondial)	Mondial
1950	Bruno Ruffo (Italian, Mondial)	Mondial
1951	Carlo Ubbiali (Italian, Mondial)	Mondial
1952	Cecil Sandford (British, MV Agusta)	MV Agusta
1953	Werner Haas (West German, NSU)	NSU
1954	Rupert Hollaus (Austrian, NSU)	NSU
1955	Carlo Ubbiali (Italian, MV Agusta)	MV Agusta
1956	Carlo Ubbiali (Italian, MV Agusta)	MV Agusta
1957	Tarquinio Provini (Italian, Mondial)	Mondial
1958	Carlo Ubbiali (Italian, MV Agusta)	MV Agusta
1959	Carlo Ubbiali (Italian, MV Agusta)	MV Agusta
1960	Carlo Ubbiali (Italian, MV Agusta)	MV Agusta
1961	Tom Phillis (Australian, Honda)	Honda
1962	Luigi Taveri (Swiss, Honda)	Honda
1963	Hugh Anderson (New Zealand, Suzuki)	Suzuki
1964	Luigi Taveri (Swiss, Honda)	Honda
1965	Hugh Anderson (New Zealand, Suzuki)	Suzuki
1966	Luigi Taveri (Swiss, Honda)	Honda
1967	Bill Ivy (British, Yamaha)	Yamaha
1968	Phil Read (British, Yamaha)	Yamaha
1969	Dave Simmonds (British, Kawasaki)	Kawasaki
1970	Dieter Braun (West German, Suzuki)	Suzuki
1971	Angel Nieto (Spanish, Derbi)	Derbi
1972	Angel Nieto (Spanish, Derbi)	Derbi
1973	Kent Andersson (Swedish, Yamaha)	Yamaha
1974	Kent Andersson (Swedish, Yamaha)	Yamaha
1975	Paolo Pileri Bianchi (Italian, Morbidelli)	Morbidelli
1976	Pier Paolo Bianchi (Italian, Morbidelli)	Morbidelli
1977	Pier Paolo Bianchi (Italian, Morbidelli)	Morbidelli
1978	Eugenio Lazzarini (Italian, MBA)	MBA
1979	Angel Nieto (Spanish, Minarelli)	Minarelli
1980	Pier Paolo Bianchi (Italian, MBA)	MBA
1981	Angel Nieto (Spanish, Minarelli)	Minarelli
1982	Angel Nieto (Spanish, Garelli)	Garelli
1983	Angel Nieto (Spanish, Garelli)	Garelli
1984	Angel Nieto (Spanish, Garelli)	Garelli
1985	Fausto Gresini (Italian, Garelli)	Garelli
1986	Luca Cadalora (Italian, Garelli)	Garelli
1987	Fausto Gresini (Italian, Garelli)	Garelli
1988	Jorge Martinez (Spanish, Derbi)	Derbi
1989	Alex Criville (Spanish, Cobas)	Cobas
1990	Loris Capirossi (Italian, Honda)	Honda

PAST SIDECAR WORLD CHAMPIONS

YEAR	RIDER	MANUFACTURER
1949	E. Oliver, D. Jenkinson (British)	Norton
1950	E. Oliver (British), L. Dobelli (Italian)	Norton
1951	E. Oliver (British), L. Dobelli (Italian)	Norton
1952	C. Smith, B. Clements (British)	Norton
1953	E. Oliver, S. Dibben (British)	Norton
1954	W. Noll, F. Cron (West German)	BMW
1955	W. Faust, K. Remmert (West German)	BMW
1956	W. Noll, F. Cron (West German)	BMW
1957	F. Hillebrand, M. Grunwald (West German)	BMW
1958	W. Schneider, H. Strauss (West German)	BMW
1959	W. Schneider, H. Strauss (West German)	BMW
1960	H. Fath, A. Wohligemuth (West German)	BMW
1961	M. Deubel, E.Horner (West German)	BMW
1962	M. Deubel, E. Horner (West German)	BMW
1963	M. Deubel, E. Horner (West German)	BMW
1964	M. Deubel, E. Horner (West German)	BMW
1965	F. Scheidegger (Swiss), J. Robinson (British)	BMW
1966	F. Scheidegger (Swiss), J. Robinson (British)	BMW
1967	K. Enders, R. Engelhardt (West German)	BMW
1968	H. Fath, W. Kallaugh (West German)	URS
1969	K. Enders, R. Engelhardt (West German)	BMW
1970	K. Enders, W. Kallaugh (West German)	BMW
1971	H. Owesle (German), P. Rutterford (British)	URS Fath
1972	K. Enders, R. Engelhardt (West German)	BMW
1973	K. Enders, R. Engelhardt (West German)	BMW
1974	K. Enders, R. Engelhardt (West German)	Bosch BMW
1975	R. Steinhausen, J. Huber (West German)	Bosch Konig
1976	R. Steinhausen, J. Huber (West German)	Bosch Konig
1977	G. O'Dell, K. Arthur, C. Holland (British)	Yamaha
1978	R. Biland (Swiss), K. Williams (British)	Yamaha
1979	B2A R. Biland, K. Waltisperg (Swiss)	Yamaha
1979	B2B B. Holzer, K. Meierhans (Swiss)	Yamaha
1980	J. Taylor (British), B. Johansson (Swedish)	Yamaha
1981	R. Biland, K. Waltisperg (Swiss)	Yamaha
1982	W. Schwarzel, A. Huber (West German)	Yamaha
1983	R. Biland, K. Waltisperg (Swiss)	Yamaha
1984	E. Streuer, B. Schnieders (Dutch)	Yamaha
1985	E. Streuer, B. Schnieders (Dutch)	Yamaha
1986	E. Streuer, B. Schnieders (Dutch)	Yamaha
1987	S. Webster, T. Hewitt (British)	Yamaha
1988	S. Webster, T. Hewitt (British)	Krauser
1989	S. Webster, T. Hewitt (British)	Krauser
1990	A. Michel (French), S. Birchall (British)	Krauser

INDEX

Individual motorcycles are listed under manufacturer or designer. Page references in italics are to illustrations.

ACKNOWLEDGEMENTS

All Sport Photographic: pp8/9; 26; 27c. BMW (UK) Ltd: p41. D Broadbend: p124. Kel Edge: pp116/117; 119tr. Paul Garson and Roy Kidney: p89. David Goldman: p125r. Patrick Gosling: pp11b; 47; 79b. Honda (UK) Ltd: p21b. Illustrated Encyclopedia of Motorcycles, edited by Erwin Tragatsen: pp6/7, 52/53; 109l. Kawasaki Motors (UK) Ltd: pp21tr; 21tl; 109r; 111. Welton Lane: p33b. Welton Lane and Oli Tennant: pp99; 101. Julian Mackie: pp11t; 37bl; 43; 45l; 45tr; 45br; 71; 83. Mitsui Yamaha: pp22; 23tl; 84/85; 107tr; 114/115. Andrew Morland: pp24c, 39 inset. Don Morley: pp16; 17tl; 18/19; 38c. Rothman's Honda: p97. Superbike Magazine: pp11b; 14/15; 22; 23tr; 24t; 24tr; 25b; 31; 35; 47bl; 47t; 55; 57; 59; 61; 63; 69tr; 73b; 87; 104/105; 108; 118r; 119br; 122/123. Suzuki Motor: pp22/23c. Oli Tennant: pp10; 28; 29; 33t; 37tr; 37tl; 37br; 45cr; 51; 65; 69cl; 73t; 75; 77; 79t; 81; 91; 93; 95; 103; 125l.

t = top; b = bottom; c = centre; l = left; r = right